SUNLY
REFLECTION
DREW KELECHI

CRYPTIC COMPOSITION
V1.1

Dedication

My younger brother inspired the development of portions of this book. By age 17, he had earned a license that allowed him to fly private planes by himself. Shortly afterwards, he earned three congressional nominations to the United States Air Force Academy. Among many other things, he's a subject matter expert in software development.

Contents

Words of Wisdom

Respect your elders.
Believe in yourself at all costs.
Seek goodness in your neighbor.
Strive to think good thoughts.

Author's Note

This artifact is a learning supplement for
SHUT UP! Nobody Likes You.

SUNLY
REFLECTION

NIGHTMARES: INTERVENTION

Discussion Questions

Note: Selected answers are located in the
"Confessions" section.

1. Whenever it came time to break into pairs during
   class, Drew was always the "odd man out." This
   trend eventually became the subject of cruel
   jokes and name-calling.

   a. Put yourself in Drew's shoes during class.
      What are some of the thoughts going through
      your head?
   b. Assume the role of a bystander. How do you
      feel hearing the cruel jokes? How might you
      positively redirect others?
   c. Have you witnessed or experienced anything
      similar?

2. Everybody at school and in the neighborhood
   eagerly anticipated Tanner's sixth birthday
   party. The day before the party, Tanner yelled
   across the neighborhood to Drew, "Guess what?
   I'm having a birthday party tomorrow, and you're
   not invited!"

a. How would this statement make you feel?

b. What could have been going through Tanner's mind when he said this?

c. Is it possible that Tanner's parents were responsible for his words?

3. In the boarding house described in chapter 9, Drew's fellow students beat him ruthlessly several times a week. He didn't inform the boarding house master or teachers because the boys would have labelled him a "snitch" and dealt with him behind the backs of the adults. Kids in the boarding house were also not afforded the luxury of calling home or contacting their parents.

a. What would you do in Drew's shoes?

b. As a bystander in boarding house witnessing the frequent beatings, what effective strategy might you use to intervene? How might you suggest more appropriate behavior to students?

4. In chapter 5, Drew describes approaching a table in the cafeteria during lunch. As soon as he put his lunch tray down, the other students at the tables whispered together, then everybody vacated the table. Several witnesses laughed mockingly.

a. What are some of the thoughts and feelings Drew may have experienced at that moment?

b. As a bystander witnessing the incident, how would you respond?

c. Have you witnessed or experienced anything similar?

5. In chapter 3, Drew says that Aunt Candace banned children from all family parties, including New Year's, the 4th of July, Christmas, and birthdays. When Aunt Candace eventually had children, they were always included.

a. Why was the "no children" mandate from Aunt Candace especially hurtful to Drew?

b. How would you feel in Drew's position?

6. In chapter 3, Aunt Candace sent Drew's family a Christmas card depicting her standing next to her new exotic car. Inside the card, she described a $15,000 watch that she had just purchased for her husband.

a. What gifts did Aunt Candace send Drew that Christmas?

b. Does this seem hurtful? Why or why not? (discuss)

c. Why do you think Aunt Candace did this?

7. In chapter 4, Drew was a fifth grader. Aunt Candace instructed Drew and his brother to each write lists of five things they wanted for Christmas. She promised to get them two things from each list and assured them that there was no price restriction.

a. Did Aunt Candace deliver on her promise?

b. What gifts did Drew and Micah receive?

c. How would you respond if you were in Drew's shoes?

8. In chapter 2, Drew writes about playing catch with Uncle Greg in his backyard. Five minutes into their game, Aunt Candace appeared on the back porch and told Uncle Greg that he didn't have to play with Drew.

a. Put yourself in Uncle Greg's shoes. How would you have responded?

b. How would you feel if you were in Drew's shoes?

9. In chapter 1, Drew writes that when Mommy and Daddy first started dating, Grandma Lucy learned of Daddy's race and nearly disowned her daughter.

a. What thoughts might have been going through Grandma Lucy's head?

b. Could Grandma Lucy's upbringing have been a factor? Explain.

10. When Grandma Lucy receives an invitation to Mommy and Daddy's wedding in chapter 1, she declines, saying that she planned to go on vacation with a friend the week of the wedding.

a. Which was a priority, the wedding or the vacation?

b. Should the wedding have been a priority? Why or why not?

11. In chapter 1, Drew writes that while Mommy was pregnant with Drew, Daddy called Grandma Lucy "Grandma." What was Grandma Lucy's response?

12. What was so hurtful about the name Aunt Candace gave to her first daughter, Sarah, in chapter 3?

13. On the sidelines during the lacrosse scrimmage that Drew describes in chapter 3, Dave took off his helmet and shook his long blonde hair from side to side. Dave then looked at Drew's hair, which carried the imprint of his helmet, and jeeringly asked if he could shake out his hair.

   a. How would you feel in Drew's shoes?
   b. Imagine yourself as a bystander. How would you respond?

14. In chapter 3, Drew says that during PE class, Mr. Dillon instructed his students to break into pairs. When Drew discretely asked Mr. Dillon to be his partner, he responded, "Oh wow, buddy. Isn't that what your friends are for? … You sure are a sorry fellow, aren't you?"

   a. What could the teacher have done differently?
   b. What would have been a more helpful response from the teacher?

c. If the teacher had responded differently,
    would the students have responded
    differently?
d. What's a better way to pair kids that avoids
    excluding anyone?

15. In chapter 3, Mrs. Taylor was upset with Drew.
    After class, she followed him to his next class
    and informed the substitute teacher about Drew.

    a. How do you think Drew and his classmates felt
        hearing her words?
    b. How would you respond if you were the
        substitute teacher?

16. In chapter 3, during handwriting lessons, Jeff
    mentioned to the class that the tenth graders
    were calling Drew "The Skater." Christopher
    became angry at this news, saying, "Hey, Drew.
    How 'bout you stop being a stupid showoff and
    get some friends." Dave added, "Ha! You see what
    I've been saying, dude? Everyone hates you,
    Drew, you frizzy-headed freak." The teacher was
    present in the room.

    a. What was the teacher's response to
        Christopher and Dave?
    b. When Drew finally responded to Christopher
        and Dave, what was the teacher's response to
        Drew?
    c. Why might the teacher have responded the way
        he did?

17. When Drew was in fifth grade, which he writes about in chapter 3, the only times Drew didn't wear a hat or hoodie was when he was in class.

    a. How did he feel about his hair?
    b. Why did he feel this way?

18. Whenever someone told a hilarious joke in class, all the kids would laugh together. As soon as Dave spotted Drew laughing at the joke, he would signal for everyone to stop laughing and say, "Why are you laughing, Drew? Nobody likes you here!" The class would hear this and resume laughing, but now their laughter was directed at Drew.

    a. How would you feel in Drew's position?
    b. How would you react to this scenario as a bystander?

19. During lacrosse games, Drew's teammates would boo or roll their eyes whenever he scored a goal. Even at the expense of forfeiting points, they would never pass him the ball. The coaches turned a blind eye to their behavior, which effectively sanctioned their bullying.

    a. How would you react as a member of the team witnessing such behavior?
    b. As a witness, would you respond? Why or why not?
    c. How could the coaches best handle this situation?

Confessions

SELECTED ANSWERS:

1.

    a. (discuss)
    b. (discuss)
    c. (discuss)

2.

    a. (discuss)
    b. (discuss)
    c. (discuss)

3.

    a. (discuss)
    b. (discuss)

4.

    a. (discuss)
    b. (discuss)
    c. (discuss)

5.

    a. Drew and his brother were the only children in the family at the time. Aunt Candace's "no children" mandate translated into "no mixed kids allowed."
    b. (discuss)

6.

    a. Used and damaged computer games discarded from Uncle Greg's home office.
    b. (discuss)
    c. (discuss)

7.

    a. No
    b. Crayons
    c. (discuss)

8.
  a. (discuss)
  b. (discuss)

9.
  a. (discuss)
  b. (discuss)

10.
  a. (discuss)
  b. (discuss)

11.
Grandma Lucy exploded in a fit of anger, warning Daddy that her name was Lucy and nothing more.

12.
Sarah was the name of Drew's deceased infant sister. Aunt Candace intentionally used the name to hurt Drew's parents, and when questioned, she said, "It's just a name we liked."

13.
  a. (discuss)
  b. (discuss)

14.
  a. (discuss)
  b. (discuss)
  c. (discuss)
  d. (discuss)

15.
  a. (discuss)
  b. (discuss)

16.
  a. The teacher pretended to bury his face in a newspaper.
  b. The teacher immediately rose to his feet and scolded Drew, saying, "Excuse me, Drew! Who do

you think you are, talking to people like
that? Go to the principal's office now!"
c. (discuss)

17.
a. He felt that his hair was abnormal. On p. 38,
Drew writes, "I felt like I had a disgusting,
spongy parasite permanently latched onto my
head, dooming me to eternal friendlessness."
b. (discuss)

18.
a. (discuss)
b. (discuss)

19.
a. (discuss)
b. (discuss)
c. (discuss)

< V C.

CRYPTIC COMPOSITION

INSTRUCTIONS:

1. Cut each page along the dotted lines labeled "cut."
2. Fold your cut-out page over the dotted line labeled "fold."
3. Insert a single 3x5 index card into the folded page. The longest edge of the index card should be flush against the back of the line labeled "fold."
4. Trim any excess page around the index card.
5. Use clear tape to affix the cut-out page to the index card.
6. Congratulations! You have just made a Cryptic Composition Flash Card.
7. Keep your Cryptic Composition Flash Card as a reference.

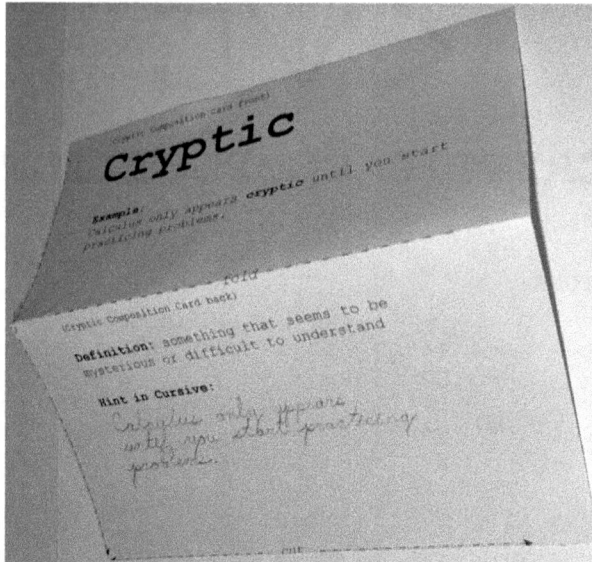

(Cryptic Composition card front)

Cryptic

Example:
Calculus only appears **cryptic** until you start practicing problems.

(Cryptic Composition Card back)

Definition: something that seems to be mysterious or difficult to understand

Hint in Cursive:

Calculus only appears until you start practicing problems.

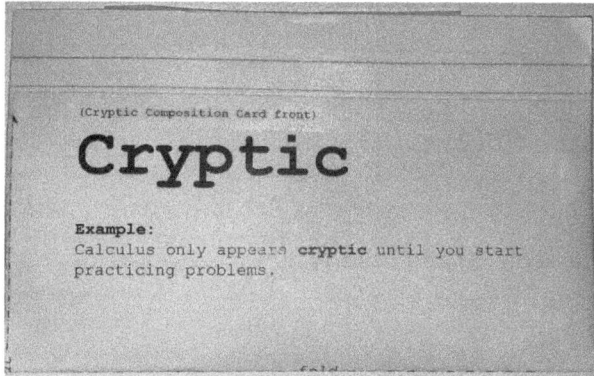

(Cryptic Composition Card front)

Cryptic

Example:
Calculus only appears **cryptic** until you start practicing problems.

DISCLAIMER: Words often have more than one meaning. If you truly want to become a wordsmith, research the different meanings of the vocabulary word listed on each Cryptic Composition Flash Card.

Cryptic Verbiage

Cryptic

Example:
Calculus only appears **cryptic** until you start
practicing problems.

- - - - - - - - - - - *fold* - - - - - - - - - - -

Definition: something that seems to be mysterious or
difficult to understand

Hint in Cursive:

Calculus only appears ▮▮▮▮▮▮
until you start practicing
problems.

Pull top of page toward you, folding across the line below.

- - - - - - - - - - - *fold* - - - - - - - - - -

Excess

Example:
Gautfred consumed dessert in **excess** and developed a
tummy ache.

- - - - - - - - - - - *fold* - - - - - - - - - - -

Definition: more than what is needed or usual

Hint in Cursive:

Gautfred consumed dessert in
▨▨▨▨▨▨ and developed a
tummy ache.

Pull top of page toward you, folding across the line below.

- - - - - - - - - - - *fold* - - - - - - - - - -

Affix

Example:

Florian likes to **affix** skateboard stickers to the
front door of his home.

- - - - - - - - - - - *fold* - - - - - - - - - -

Definition: to physically attach

Hint in Cursive:

Florian likes to ▓▓▓▓▓▓▓
*skateboard stickers to the
front door of his home.*

Pull top of page toward you, folding across the line below.

- - - - - - - - - - - - *fold* - - - - - - - - - - -

Disclaimer

Example:
Before singing on stage, Norbert issued a **disclaimer** to the audience about the strobe lights he used in his act.

- - - - - - - - - - - - *fold* - - - - - - - - - -

Definition: a statement that denies responsibility or liability

Hint in Cursive:

Before singing on stage, Norbert issued a _____ *to the audience about the strobe lights he used in his act.*

Pull top of page toward you, folding across the line below.

- - - - - - - - - - - - *fold* - - - - - - - - - - -

Academia

Example:
In **academia,** people work together to learn and share
knowledge.

- - - - - - - - - - - *fold* - - - - - - - - - - -

Definition: the world of education and schools

Hint in Cursive:

*In ＿＿＿＿＿＿, people work
together to learn and share
knowledge.*

Pull top of page toward you, folding across the line below.

- - - - - - - - - - - - *fold* - - - - - - - - - - -

Measly

Example:

Olaf grew annoyed when the restaurant served him a **measly** portion of meat.

- - - - - - - - - - - - *fold* - - - - - - - - - - -

Definition: very small or of little importance

Hint in Cursive:

Olaf grew annoyed when the restaurant served him a _____ portion of meat.

cut

cut

cut

cut

Pull top of page toward you, folding across the line below.

- - - - - - - - - - - *fold* - - - - - - - - - -

Leverage

Example:
Malena wants to **leverage** her computer skills to teach
her grandparents how to use macros.

- - - - - - - - - - - - *fold* - - - - - - - - - - -

Definition: to use for advantage or gain; using small
effort to achieve a large result

Hint in Cursive:

Malena wants to [_____]
her computer skills to teach her
grandparents how to use macros.

Pull top of page toward you, folding across the line below.

- - - - - - - - - - - - *fold* - - - - - - - - - - -

Utter

Example:
Torkel watched in **utter** disbelief as the chef served him a child-sized portion of stew.

- - - - - - - - - - fold - - - - - - - - - -

Definition: taken to the highest level or extreme point

Hint in Cursive:

Torkel watched in ▮▮▮▮▮ disbelief as the chef served him a child-sized portion of stew.

31

Pull top of page toward you, folding across the line below.

- - - - - - - - - - - *fold* - - - - - - - - - -

Facet

Example:

Fritigern's favorite **facet** of math is trigonometry.

- - - - - - - - - - - - - *fold* - - - - - - - - - - -

Definition: one side or aspect of something

Hint in Cursive:

Fritigern's favorite ███████████ *of math is trigonometry.*

Pull top of page toward you, folding across the line below.

- - - - - - - - - - - *fold* - - - - - - - - - -

Enumerate

Example:

Whenever their mother refuses to buy candy, Gildas and Catrin **enumerate** the reasons they deserve a treat.

- - - - - - - - - - - *fold* - - - - - - - - - - -

Definition: to count or list things one by one

Hint in Cursive:

Whenever their mother refuses to buy candy, Gildas and Catrin _____ the reasons they deserve a treat.

Pull top of page toward you, folding across the line below.

- - - - - - - - - - - *fold* - - - - - - - - - -

Savvy

Example:

Ever the **savvy** shopper, Ambrosius waited for a sale before purchasing his lacrosse helmet.

- - - - - - - - - - - *fold* - - - - - - - - - -

Definition: having practical knowledge or understanding

Hint in Cursive:

Ever the _____ shopper, Ambrosius waited for a sale before purchasing his lacrosse helmet.

Pull top of page toward you, folding across the line below.

- - - - - - - - - - - - *fold* - - - - - - - - - -

Intrigued

Example:
Intrigued by a paper she read on rocket science, Rosamund began studying physics and chemistry.

See p. 35 of *SHUT UP! Nobody Likes You* for additional usage.

- - - - - - - - - - - *fold* - - - - - - - - - -

Definition: interested and curious about something

Hint in Cursive:

░░░░░░░░ *by a paper she read on rocket science, Rosamund began studying physics and chemistry.*

Pull top of page toward you, folding across the line below.

- - - - - - - - - - - *fold* - - - - - - - - - -

Pitch

Example:

After annoying his mother, Hengist needed an excellent sales **pitch** to convince her to lend him $25.

- - - - - - - - - - - *fold* - - - - - - - - - - -

Definition: a sales presentation

Hint in Cursive:

After annoying his mother, Hengist needed an excellent sales _____ to convince her to lend him $25.

Pull top of page toward you, folding across the line below.

- - - - - - - - - - - *fold* - - - - - - - - - -

Articulate

Example:

The teacher offered Vetranio extra credit to **articulate** his point of view during class.

- - - - - - - - - - - fold - - - - - - - - - -

Definition: expressing thoughts clearly in words

Hint in Cursive:

The teacher offered Vetranio extra credit to _____ his point of view during class.

Pull top of page toward you, folding across the line below.

- - - - - - - - - - - *fold* - - - - - - - - - -

Patron

Example:
In line for Chinese food, Nennius filled up on free beef samples provided to each **patron**.

- - - - - - - - - - - fold - - - - - - - - - -

Definition: a person who supports or gives financial assistance to someone or something

Hint in Cursive:

In line for Chinese food, Nennius filled up on free beef samples provided to each ⬜⬜⬜⬜⬜ .

Pull top of page toward you, folding across the line below.

- - - - - - - - - - - *fold* - - - - - - - - - -

Lambaste

Example:

I wore mismatched gym shoes to the dance, and my friends didn't hesitate to **lambaste** me for the silly decision.

- - - - - - - - - - - *fold* - - - - - - - - - -

Definition: to criticize or scold very strongly

Hint in Cursive:

I wore mismatched gym shoes to the dance, and my friends didn't hesitate to _____ me for the silly decision.

Pull top of page toward you, folding across the line below.

- - - - - - - - - - - *fold* - - - - - - - - - -

Stifle

Example:

I fought to **stifle** my laughs as Tilghman made silly
faces at me during the calculus examination.

See p. 95 of *SHUT UP! Nobody Likes You* for additional
usage.

- - - - - - - - - - *fold* - - - - - - - - - -

(Cryptic Composition Card back)

Definition: to withhold from circulation or expression

Hint in Cursive:

*I fought to ▓▓▓▓▓ my laughs
as Tilghman made silly faces
at me during the calculus
examination.*

Pull top of page toward you, folding across the line below.

- - - - - - - - - - - *fold* - - - - - - - - - -

Primitive

Example:
Cenwald and his sisters displayed **primitive** behavior
by yelling and running through the mall.

See p. 103 *of SHUT UP! Nobody Likes You* for additional
usage.

- - - - - - - - - - - *fold* - - - - - - - - - -

Definition: outdated, uncivilized, or lacking in
sophistication

Hint in Cursive:

Cenwald and his sisters displayed ▨▨▨▨▨▨ behavior by yelling and running through the mall.

Pull top of page toward you, folding across the line below.

- - - - - - - - - - - *fold* - - - - - - - - - -

Exasperate

Example:

The server would **exasperate** Leodegar anytime she brought a dish that didn't include the amount of meat he paid for.

See p. 103 of *SHUT UP! Nobody Likes You* for additional usage.

- - - - - - - - - - - *fold* - - - - - - - - - -

(Cryptic Composition Card back)

Definition: to cause extreme irritation, annoyance, or frustration

Hint in Cursive:

The server would ▓▓▓▓▓▓▓ Leodegar anytime she brought a dish that didn't include the amount of meat he paid for.

Pull top of page toward you, folding across the line below.

- - - - - - - - - - - *fold* - - - - - - - - - -

Persuade

Example:
Vittorio couldn't **persuade** his calculus teacher to allow an extra twenty minutes on the test.

See p. 2 of *SHUT UP! Nobody Likes You* for additional usage.

- - - - - - - - - - - *fold* - - - - - - - - - -

(Cryptic Composition Card back)

Definition: to convince or make someone agree with you

Hint in Cursive:

Vittorio couldn't ▮▮▮▮▮ his calculus teacher to allow an extra twenty minutes on the test.

Pull top of page toward you, folding across the line below.

- - - - - - - - - - - *fold* - - - - - - - - - -

Elated

Example:

After winning the tournament, the **elated** baseball team cheered and jumped for joy.

See p. 4 of *SHUT UP! Nobody Likes You* for additional usage.

- - - - - - - - - - - fold - - - - - - - - - - -

(Cryptic Composition Card back)

Definition: extremely happy or joyful

Hint in Cursive:

After winning the tournament, the _____ baseball team cheered and jumped for joy.

Pull top of page toward you, folding across the line below.

- - - - - - - - - - - *fold* - - - - - - - - - -

(Cryptic Composition Card front)

Degrade

Example:
People often **degrade** criminal offenders who have been released from prison.

See p. 4 of *SHUT UP! Nobody Likes You* for additional usage.

- - - - - - - - - - - - *fold* - - - - - - - - - - - -

(Cryptic Composition Card back)

Definition: to treat someone with disrespect, lower their value

Hint in Cursive:

People often ________ criminal offenders who have been released from prison.

cut

cut

cut

Pull top of page toward you, folding across the line below.

- - - - - - - - - - - - - *fold* - - - - - - - - - - - -

Neglect

Example:
The outcome of Beltran's academic **neglect** was a poor grade on the quiz.

See p. 6 of *SHUT UP! Nobody Likes You* for additional usage.

- - - - - - - - - - - *fold* - - - - - - - - - -

(Cryptic Composition Card back)

Definition: fail to take care of or pay attention to something or someone

Hint in Cursive:

The outcome of Beltran's academic _____ was a poor grade on the quiz.

Pull top of page toward you, folding across the line below.

- - - - - - - - - - - - *fold* - - - - - - - - - -

Orchestrate

Example:
Petronilla worked with her family members to **orchestrate** Mom's surprise birthday party.

See p. 7 of *SHUT UP! Nobody Likes You* for additional usage.

- - - - - - - - - - - fold - - - - - - - - - -

(Cryptic Composition Card back)

Definition: to organize or arrange things, especially a complex event

Hint in Cursive:

Petronilla worked with her family members to _____ Mom's surprise birthday party.

Pull top of page toward you, folding across the line below.

- - - - - - - - - - - - *fold* - - - - - - - - - - -

Encounter

Example:

When Thrasamund and his sister trek through the dense forest, they often **encounter** brown bears.

See p. 8 of *SHUT UP! Nobody Likes You* for additional usage.

- - - - - - - - - - - *fold* - - - - - - - - - -

(Cryptic Composition Card back)

Definition: to meet or come across someone or something

Hint in Cursive:

When Thrasamund and his sister trek through the dense forest, they often _____ brown bears.

Pull top of page toward you, folding across the line below.

- - - - - - - - - - - *fold* - - - - - - - - - -

Resent

Example:
His mother's insistence that he redo his sloppy
handwriting caused Benvolio to **resent** her all morning.

See p. 8 of *SHUT UP! Nobody Likes You* for additional
usage.
- - - - - - - - - - - *fold* - - - - - - - - - -
(Cryptic Composition Card back)

Definition: to feel bitterness or anger about
something, especially an injustice

Hint in Cursive:

*His mother's insistence that he redo
his sloppy handwriting caused
Benvolio to _____ her all
morning.*

Pull top of page toward you, folding across the line below.

- - - - - - - - - - - - *fold* - - - - - - - - - - -

Lukewarm

Example:

After receiving socks for Christmas instead of the skateboard he was promised, Baldwin gave a **lukewarm** "thank you" to his aunt.

See p. 8 of *SHUT UP! Nobody Likes You* for additional usage.

- - - - - - - - - - - fold - - - - - - - - - -

(Cryptic Composition Card back)

Definition: lacking enthusiasm or interest

Hint in Cursive:

After receiving socks for Christmas instead of the skateboard he was promised, Baldwin gave a ▓▓▓▓▓▓▓▓ "thank you" to his aunt.

cut

69

Pull top of page toward you, folding across the line below.

- - - - - - - - - - - - *fold* - - - - - - - - - - -

Slight

Example:
Refusing a handshake is a **slight** that usually upsets people.

See p. 8 of *SHUT UP! Nobody Likes You* for additional usage.

- - - - - - - - - - - *fold* - - - - - - - - - -
(Cryptic Composition Card back)

Definition: to treat with disrespect or disregard

Hint in Cursive:

Refusing a handshake is a ▓▓▓▓▓▓ that usually upsets people.

Pull top of page toward you, folding across the line below.

- - - - - - - - - - - - fold - - - - - - - - - - - -

Hostile

Example:
After being caught in a lie, Leofric became **hostile** and yelled at the reporter.

See p. 8 of *SHUT UP! Nobody Likes You* for additional usage.

- - - - - - - - - - - *fold* - - - - - - - - - -

(Cryptic Composition Card back)

Definition: unfriendly, aggressive, or antagonistic

Hint in Cursive:

After being caught in a lie, Leofrick became _____ and yelled at the reporter.

Pull top of page toward you, folding across the line below.

- - - - - - - - - - - *fold* - - - - - - - - - -

Prone

Example:

Sigebert held his grandmother's hand as she walked down the icy walkway because she was **prone** to falling without her cane.

See p. 9 of *SHUT UP! Nobody Likes You* for additional usage.

- - - - - - - - - - - - *fold* - - - - - - - - - -

(Cryptic Composition Card back)

Definition: likely to experience or suffer from something

Hint in Cursive:

Sigebert held his grandmother's hand as she walked down the icy walkway because she was ▓▓▓▓▓▓▓ to falling without her cane.

cut

75

Pull top of page toward you, folding across the line below.

- - - - - - - - - - - *fold* - - - - - - - - - -

Lavish

Example:
The day after she left for the beach, Volkmar and his friends used his aunt's castle to host **lavish** dinner parties.

See p. 9 of *SHUT UP! Nobody Likes You* for additional usage.
- - - - - - - - - - - fold - - - - - - - - - -

Definition: generous, extravagant, or abundant

Hint in Cursive:

The day after she left for the beach, Volkmar and his friends used his aunts castle to host _____ dinner parties.

Pull top of page toward you, folding across the line below.

- - - - - - - - - - - - *fold* - - - - - - - - - - -

Sprawling

Example:

Atop the mountain, Adhemar observed the **sprawling** woodlands and beautiful, fruited plains.

See p. 9 of *SHUT UP! Nobody Likes You* for additional usage.

- - - - - - - - - - - *fold* - - - - - - - - - -

(Cryptic Composition Card back)

Definition: extending over a large area

Hint in Cursive:

Atop the mountain, Adhemar observed the woodlands and beautiful fruited plains.

Pull top of page toward you, folding across the line below.

- - - - - - - - - - - *fold* - - - - - - - - - -

Excruciating

Example:
After an intense gym class, waiting in line for the water fountain was an **excruciating** test of patience for Ingjald.

See p. 9 of *SHUT UP! Nobody Likes You* for additional usage.

- - - - - - - - - - - - fold - - - - - - - - - - -

(Cryptic Composition Card back)

Definition: extremely painful or intense

Hint in Cursive:

After an intense gym class, waiting in line for the water fountain was an _____ test of patience for Ingjald.

- - - - - - - - - - - - cut - - - - - - - - - - -

Pull top of page toward you, folding across the line below.

- - - - - - - - - - - - *fold* - - - - - - - - - - -

Shun

Example:

Archibald and his brother **shun** mashed potatoes anytime their father serves meatloaf.

See p. 9 of *SHUT UP! Nobody Likes You* for additional usage.

- - - - - - - - - - - fold - - - - - - - - - -

Definition: to avoid or deliberately ignore someone or something

Hint in Cursive:

Archibald and his brother ▓▓▓▓▓ mashed potatoes anytime their father serves meatloaf.

Pull top of page toward you, folding across the line below.

- - - - - - - - - - - *fold* - - - - - - - - - -

(Cryptic Composition Card front)

Grouse

Example:
Diggory enjoys candy, but he starts to **grouse** when it's time to eat green beans.

See p. 10 of *SHUT UP! Nobody Likes You* for additional usage.

cut

- - - - - - - - - - - - *fold* - - - - - - - - - - -

cut

(Cryptic Composition Card back)

Definition: to complain or grumble

Hint in Cursive:

Diggory enjoys candy, but he starts to ___ when it's time to eat green beans.

cut

Pull top of page toward you, folding across the line below.

- - - - - - - - - - - *fold* - - - - - - - - - -

Relentless

Example:

After earning a C on her mid-term, Desideria was **relentless** in her studies, and she fought her way back to an A.

See p. 10 of *SHUT UP! Nobody Likes You* for additional usage.

- - - - - - - - - - - - fold - - - - - - - - - -

Definition: persistent, continuous, and unyielding

Hint in Cursive:

After earning a C on her mid-term, Desideria was _____ in her studies, and she fought her way back to an A.

Pull top of page toward you, folding across the line below.

- - - - - - - - - - - *fold* - - - - - - - - - - -

Reluctant

Example:
Balthasar was **reluctant** to paint his cousin's castle for free.

See p. 10 of *SHUT UP! Nobody Likes You* for additional usage.
- - - - - - - - - - - - *fold* - - - - - - - - - -
(Cryptic Composition Card back)

Definition: unwilling or hesitant to do something

Hint in Cursive:

Balthasar was _____ to paint his cousin's castle for free.

Pull top of page toward you, folding across the line below.

- - - - - - - - - - - - *fold* - - - - - - - - - -

Overt

Example:
Eadwig mocked his teacher, showing **overt** disrespect.

See p. 10 of *SHUT UP! Nobody Likes You* for additional usage.
- - - - - - - - - - - fold - - - - - - - - - -
(Cryptic Composition Card back)

Definition: open, not hidden, and easily observed

Hint in Cursive:

Eadwig mocked his teacher, showing _____ disrespect.

Pull top of page toward you, folding across the line below.

- - - - - - - - - - - *fold* - - - - - - - - - -

Exclude

Example:
The neighborhood threw an "adults only" party to
exclude all children.

See p. 10 of *SHUT UP! Nobody Likes You* for additional
usage.
- - - - - - - - - - - - *fold* - - - - - - - - - -
(Cryptic Composition Card back)

Definition: to leave out or not include someone or
something

Hint in Cursive:

*The neighborhood threw an "adults
only" party to ▓▓▓▓▓▓▓▓▓▓ all children.*

- - - - - - - - - - - - - - - *cut* - - - - - - - - - - - - - - -

93

Pull top of page toward you, folding across the line below.

- - - - - - - - - - - - *fold* - - - - - - - - - - -

Taint

Example:
After Fulbert accidentally dropped his cup on his mother's white couch, she could never remove the grape-juice **taint.**

See p. 10 of *SHUT UP! Nobody Likes You* for additional usage.
- - - - - - - - - - - *fold* - - - - - - - - - -
(Cryptic Composition Card back)

Definition: to contaminate or pollute; spoil the purity or quality

Hint in Cursive:

After Fulbert accidentally dropped his cup on his mother's white couch, she could never remove the grape-juice _____.

Pull top of page toward you, folding across the line below.

- - - - - - - - - - - *fold* - - - - - - - - - - -

Mount

Example:
Every day after school, Thaddeus and his friends **mount** their skateboards and fly down the street.

See p. 11 of *SHUT UP! Nobody Likes You* for additional usage.

- - - - - - - - - - - *fold* - - - - - - - - - -

(Cryptic Composition Card back)

Definition: to climb or get up onto something

Hint in Cursive:

Every day after school, Thaddeus and his friends ▓▓▓▓▓▓▓ their skateboards and fly down the street.

97

Pull top of page toward you, folding across the line below.

- - - - - - - - - - - *fold* - - - - - - - - - -

Petrified

Example:

When skydiving for the first time, many are too **petrified** to jump from the plane.

See p. 11 of *SHUT UP! Nobody Likes You* for additional usage.

- - - - - - - - - - - fold - - - - - - - - - -

Definition: extremely frightened

Hint in Cursive:

When skydiving for the first time, many are too _____ to jump from the plane.

Pull top of page toward you, folding across the line below.

- - - - - - - - - - - *fold* - - - - - - - - - -

Akimbo

Example:
With arms **akimbo,** Elfrida's annoyed teacher waited for the noisy class to quiet down.

See p. 11 of *SHUT UP! Nobody Likes You* for additional usage.

- - - - - - - - - - - *fold* - - - - - - - - - -

(Cryptic Composition Card back)

Definition: with hands on hips and elbows turned outward

Hint in Cursive:

With arms ▓▓▓▓▓▓ Elfrida's annoyed teacher waited for the noisy class to quiet down.

Pull top of page toward you, folding across the line below.

- - - - - - - - - - - - *fold* - - - - - - - - - - -

Stern

Example:
After intentionally kicking the basketball into the bleachers, Millicent observed a **stern** look on her coach's face.

See p. 11 of *SHUT UP! Nobody Likes You* for additional usage.

- - - - - - - - - - - *fold* - - - - - - - - - -

(Cryptic Composition Card back)

Definition: serious, strict, and firm

Hint in Cursive:

After intentionally kicking the basketball into the bleachers, Millicent observed a _____ look on her coach's face.

Pull top of page toward you, folding across the line below.

- - - - - - - - - - - - *fold* - - - - - - - - - - -

Bellow

Example:
Whenever Laodocus grew tired, his angry drill sergeant would **bellow** commands in his face.

See p. 11 of *SHUT UP! Nobody Likes You* for additional usage.
- - - - - - - - - - - - - *fold* - - - - - - - - - - -
(Cryptic Composition Card back)

Definition: to shout loudly, often in a deep voice

Hint in Cursive:

Whenever Laodocus grew tired, his angry drill sergeant would ▓▓▓▓▓▓▓▓ commands in his face.

Pull top of page toward you, folding across the line below.

- - - - - - - - - - - - *fold* - - - - - - - - - - - -

Dumbfounded

Example:
Astrid was **dumbfounded** when her server delivered a charred ribeye after she requested rare.

See p. 11 of *SHUT UP! Nobody Likes You* for additional usage.

- - - - - - - - - - - *fold* - - - - - - - - - -

Definition: extremely surprised or shocked

Hint in Cursive:

Astrid was ▓▓▓▓▓▓▓▓ when her server delivered a charred ribeye after she requested rare.

Pull top of page toward you, folding across the line below.

- - - - - - - - - - - - *fold* - - - - - - - - - -

Malice

Example:
With a heart full of **malice**, the villain plotted to rob retirement homes.

See p. 12 of *SHUT UP! Nobody Likes You* for additional usage.

- - - - - - - - - - - *fold* - - - - - - - - - -

Definition: the intention to harm or cause pain to someone

Hint in Cursive:

*With a heart full of _____,
the villain plotted to rob
retirement homes.*

cut

Pull top of page toward you, folding across the line below.

- - - - - - - - - - - - *fold* - - - - - - - - - - -

Bewilder

Example:
Erasmus sought help from his teacher because the complicated instructions **bewilder** everyone who tries to make sense of them.

See p. 12 of *SHUT UP! Nobody Likes You* for additional usage.

- - - - - - - - - - - - fold - - - - - - - - - -

(Cryptic Composition Card back)

Definition: to confuse or puzzle someone

Hint in Cursive:

Erasmus sought help from his teacher because the complicated instructions ▓▓▓▓▓▓▓ everyone who tries to make sense of them.

Pull top of page toward you, folding across the line below.

- - - - - - - - - - - *fold* - - - - - - - - - -

Recline

Example:
Margery loved to **recline** in her beach chair, outstretching her feet and taking a deep breath of satisfaction.

See p. 12 of *SHUT UP! Nobody Likes You* for additional usage.

- - - - - - - - - - - fold - - - - - - - - - -
(Cryptic Composition Card back)

Definition: to lean back or lie down in a relaxed position

Hint in Cursive:

Margery loved to ▭ in her beach chair, outstretching her feet and taking a deep breath of satisfaction.

cut

Pull top of page toward you, folding across the line below.

- - - - - - - - - - - - *fold* - - - - - - - - - - -

Spite

Example:

As the referee declared the winner of the tournament, the losing team glared at their opponents in **spite**.

See p. 12 of *SHUT UP! Nobody Likes You* for additional usage.

- - - - - - - - - - - - *fold* - - - - - - - - - - -

Definition: malicious intention to hurt or annoy

Hint in Cursive:

As the referee declared the winner of the tournament, the losing team glared at their opponents in _____.

Pull top of page toward you, folding across the line below.

- - - - - - - - - - - *fold* - - - - - - - - - -

Deteriorate

Example:
Rain had caused the abandoned building to **deteriorate** so badly that the floors were hazardous.

See p. 12 of *SHUT UP! Nobody Likes You* for additional usage.

- - - - - - - - - - - - fold - - - - - - - - - -

(Cryptic Composition Card back)

Definition: to gradually become worse or less valuable

Hint in Cursive:

Rain had caused the abandoned building to _____ so badly that the floors were hazardous.

Pull top of page toward you, folding across the line below.

- - - - - - - - - - - - *fold* - - - - - - - - - - -

Marvel

Example:
Having never seen snow before, the African exchange
student stopped to **marvel** at the snowman standing
before him.

See p. 13 of *SHUT UP! Nobody Likes You* for additional
usage.
- - - - - - - - - - - fold - - - - - - - - - -
(Cryptic Composition Card back)

Definition: to be amazed or astonished by something

Hint in Cursive:

Having never seen snow before, the
African exchange student stopped to
_____ at the snowman
standing before him.

119

Pull top of page toward you, folding across the line below.

- - - - - - - - - - - - *fold* - - - - - - - - - - -

Willpower

Example:
Physically exhausted, Oriana relied on her **willpower** to finish the marathon.

See p. 13 of *SHUT UP! Nobody Likes You* for additional usage.

- - - - - - - - - - - *fold* - - - - - - - - - -

Definition: the ability to control one's own actions and impulses

Hint in Cursive:

Physically exhausted, Oriana relied on her _____ to finish the marathon.

Pull top of page toward you, folding across the line below.

- - - - - - - - - - - - *fold* - - - - - - - - - -

Acknowledge

Example:
During a group project, it's important to **acknowledge** the hard work and contributions of other team members.

See p. 13 of *SHUT UP! Nobody Likes You* for additional usage.

- - - - - - - - - - - fold - - - - - - - - - -

(Cryptic Composition Card back)

Definition: to recognize or admit the existence or truth of something

Hint in Cursive:

During a group project it's important to _____ the hard work and contributions of other team members.

Pull top of page toward you, folding across the line below.

- - - - - - - - - - - - *fold* - - - - - - - - - - - -

Awestruck

Example:

We were **awestruck** by the beauty of the magnificent sunset.

See p. 14 of *SHUT UP! Nobody Likes You* for additional usage.

- - - - - - - - - - - *fold* - - - - - - - - - -

(Cryptic Composition Card back)

Definition: filled with awe or amazement

Hint in Cursive:

We were ▓▓▓▓▓ by the beauty of the magnificent sunset.

Pull top of page toward you, folding across the line below.

- - - - - - - - - - - - *fold* - - - - - - - - - - -

Venture

Example:

As Arnaud prepared to **venture** into the deadly Amazon rainforest, he gathered supplies.

See p. 14 of *SHUT UP! Nobody Likes You* for additional usage.
- - - - - - - - - - - *fold* - - - - - - - - - -
(Cryptic Composition Card back)

Definition: dare to do something or take a risk

Hint in Cursive:

As Arnaud prepared to ▓▓▓▓▓ into the deadly Amazon rainforest, he gathered supplies.

Pull top of page toward you, folding across the line below.

- - - - - - - - - - - *fold* - - - - - - - - - -

Livid

Example:
The lacrosse coach was **livid** with Hrothgar's lazy
performance during the game.

See p. *14* of *SHUT UP! Nobody Likes You* for additional
usage.

- - - - - - - - - - - *fold* - - - - - - - - - -

Definition: extremely angry or furious

Hint in Cursive:

The lacrosse coach was ▓▓▓▓▓ with Hrothgar's lazy performance during the game.

Pull top of page toward you, folding across the line below.

- - - - - - - - - - - *fold* - - - - - - - - - -

Defy

Example:
Isidore and his sisters **defy** bedtime rules by playing with electronics under the covers.

See p. 14 of *SHUT UP! Nobody Likes You* for additional usage.
- - - - - - - - - - - *fold* - - - - - - - - - -
(Cryptic Composition Card back)

Definition: resist or challenge authority or rules

Hint in Cursive:

Isidore and his sisters ▓▓▓▓ bedtime rules by playing with electronics under the covers.

131

Pull top of page toward you, folding across the line below.

- - - - - - - - - - - *fold* - - - - - - - - - - -

Alienate

Example:
Using foul language to insult others can **alienate** you from your peers.

See p. 16 of *SHUT UP! Nobody Likes You* for additional usage.

- - - - - - - - - - - *fold* - - - - - - - - - -

Definition: to cause someone to feel isolated or alone

Hint in Cursive:

Using foul language to insult others can _____ you from your peers.

Pull top of page toward you, folding across the line below.

- - - - - - - - - - - - *fold* - - - - - - - - - - -

Distinct

Example:
Each student has a **distinct** personality and may have different hobbies too.

See p. 16 of *SHUT UP! Nobody Likes You* for additional usage.

- - - - - - - - - - - - fold - - - - - - - - - - - -

Definition: clearly different or separate

Hint in Cursive:

Each student has a ▓▓▓▓▓ personality and may have different hobbies too.

Pull top of page toward you, folding across the line below.

- - - - - - - - - - - - *fold* - - - - - - - - - - -

Maneuver

Example:
The skilled pilot was able to **maneuver** the aircraft
through the hurricane.

See p. 16 of *SHUT UP! Nobody Likes You* for additional
usage.
- - - - - - - - - - - *fold* - - - - - - - - - -
(Cryptic Composition Card back)

Definition: to skillfully move or guide something or
someone

Hint in Cursive:

The skilled pilot was able to ▨▨▨▨▨ the aircraft through the hurricane.

137

Pull top of page toward you, folding across the line below.

- - - - - - - - - - - - *fold* - - - - - - - - - - -

Cul-de-sac

Example:
The house was located at the end of a quiet **cul-de-sac,** providing a peaceful living environment.

See p. 16 of *SHUT UP! Nobody Likes You* for additional usage.

- - - - - - - - - - - *fold* - - - - - - - - - - -

(Cryptic Composition Card back)

Definition: a street or passage closed at one end

Hint in Cursive:

The house was located at the end of a quiet ▓▓▓▓▓▓▓, providing a peaceful living environment.

Pull top of page toward you, folding across the line below.

- - - - - - - - - - - - *fold* - - - - - - - - - -

Engross

Example:

Arabella's studies so **engross** her that she often doesn't care to go out and play.

See p. 16 of *SHUT UP! Nobody Likes You* for additional usage.

- - - - - - - - - - - - fold - - - - - - - - - -

(Cryptic Composition Card back)

Definition: to take all the attention or interest of someone

Hint in Cursive:

Arabella's studies so ▨▨▨▨▨ her that she often doesn't care to go out and play.

Pull top of page toward you, folding across the line below.

- - - - - - - - - - - *fold* - - - - - - - - - - -

(Cryptic Composition Card front)

Engage

Example:
Patroclus and his friends routinely **engage** in science experiments at school.

See p. 17 of *SHUT UP! Nobody Likes You* for additional usage.

- - - - - - - - - - - fold - - - - - - - - - -

(Cryptic Composition Card back)

Definition: to participate or become involved in something

Hint in Cursive:

Patroclus and his friends routinely _____ in science experiments at school.

143

Pull top of page toward you, folding across the line below.

- - - - - - - - - - - *fold* - - - - - - - - - -

Transfer

Example:
Gullveig only needed a few seconds to **transfer** her textbooks from her backpack to the desk.

See p. 17 of *SHUT UP! Nobody Likes You* for additional usage.
- - - - - - - - - - - fold - - - - - - - - - -
(Cryptic Composition Card back)

Definition: to move from one place to another

Hint in Cursive:

Gullveig only needed a few seconds to _____ her textbooks from her backpack to the desk.

Pull top of page toward you, folding across the line below.

- - - - - - - - - - - *fold* - - - - - - - - - -

Inordinate

Example:
Polonius added an **inordinate** amount of spice to the stew, making it extremely hot.

See p. 17 of *SHUT UP! Nobody Likes You* for additional usage.

- - - - - - - - - - - fold - - - - - - - - - -

Definition: excessive or unusually large

Hint in Cursive:

Polonius added an ▭ amount of spice to the stew, making it extremely hot.

Pull top of page toward you, folding across the line below.

- - - - - - - - - - - - *fold* - - - - - - - - - - -

(Cryptic Composition Card front)

Boast

Example:
Choosing not to **boast** about her skills, Ophelia let her performance speak for itself.

See p. 18 of *SHUT UP! Nobody Likes You* for additional usage.

- - - - - - - - - - - - *fold* - - - - - - - - - - - -

(Cryptic Composition Card back)

Definition: to talk with too much pride about one's achievements

Hint in Cursive:

Choosing not to ______ about her skills, Ophelia let her performance speak for itself.

cut

Pull top of page toward you, folding across the line below.

- - - - - - - - - - - - *fold* - - - - - - - - - - -

Afford

Example:
The vocabulary flashcards will **afford** Bernardo the opportunity to learn cool, funny words.

See p. 18 of *SHUT UP! Nobody Likes You* for additional usage.

- - - - - - - - - - - *fold* - - - - - - - - - -

(Cryptic Composition Card back)

Definition: have enough money or resources to do something

Hint in Cursive:

The vocabulary flashcards will _____ Bernardo the opportunity to learn cool, funny words.

Pull top of page toward you, folding across the line below.

- - - - - - - - - - - *fold* - - - - - - - - - -

Dedicated

Example:
Clovis was **dedicated** to perfecting the piano piece,
and he practiced hours each day.

See p. 18 of *SHUT UP! Nobody Likes You* for additional
usage.

- - - - - - - - - - - - fold - - - - - - - - - -

Definition: devoted or committed to a task or purpose

Hint in Cursive:

Clovis was _____ to perfecting the piano piece, and he practiced hours each day.

cut

Pull top of page toward you, folding across the line below.

- - - - - - - - - - - - *fold* - - - - - - - - - - -

Considerable

Example:
Heraclitus made **considerable** progress when he improved his grade from 70% to 95%.

See p. 19 of *SHUT UP! Nobody Likes You* for additional usage.
- - - - - - - - - - - *fold* - - - - - - - - - -
(Cryptic Composition Card back)

Definition: large in size, amount, or degree

Hint in Cursive:

Heraclitus made _____ progress when he improved his grade from 70% to 95%!

Pull top of page toward you, folding across the line below.

- - - - - - - - - - - *fold* - - - - - - - - - -

Strewn

Example:
Edmund played happily in the living room, his toys
strewn about.

See p. 19 of *SHUT UP! Nobody Likes You* for additional
usage.

- - - - - - - - - - - *fold* - - - - - - - - - -
(Cryptic Composition Card back)

Definition: scattered or spread untidily over a
surface

Hint in Cursive:

*Edmund played happily in
the living room, his toys
_____ about.*

157

Pull top of page toward you, folding across the line below.

- - - - - - - - - - - *fold* - - - - - - - - - -

Reconvene

Example:
Before returning to school for the spring semester,
Pericles and his friends made plans to **reconvene** in
the dining hall.

See p. 19 of *SHUT UP! Nobody Likes You* for additional
usage.

- - - - - - - - - - - - *fold* - - - - - - - - - -

Definition: to gather or assemble again, especially
after a break

Hint in Cursive:

*Before returning to school for the
spring semester, Pericles and his
friends made plans to _____
in the dining hall.*

Pull top of page toward you, folding across the line below.

- - - - - - - - - - - - *fold* - - - - - - - - - - - -

Animosity

Example:
The rival teams displayed **animosity** by taunting and fighting each other during the game.

See p. 19 of *SHUT UP! Nobody Likes You* for additional usage.

- - - - - - - - - - - *fold* - - - - - - - - - -

Definition: strong hostility or resentment

Hint in Cursive:

The rival teams displayed _____ by taunting and fighting each other during the game.

Pull top of page toward you, folding across the line below.

- - - - - - - - - - - - *fold* - - - - - - - - - - - -

Scoff

Example:
Tarquin's silly idea about building a time machine caused his father to **scoff.**

See p. 20 of *SHUT UP! Nobody Likes You* for additional usage.

- - - - - - - - - - - fold - - - - - - - - - -

(Cryptic Composition Card back)

Definition: to speak or express contempt, often in a mocking way

Hint in Cursive:

Tarquin's silly idea about building a time machine caused his father to ▬▬▬▬▬▬▬▬.

Pull top of page toward you, folding across the line below.

- - - - - - - - - - - *fold* - - - - - - - - - -

Jeer

Example:
Nabonidus loved to **jeer** at his sister whenever their mom sent her to time-out.

See p. 20 of *SHUT UP! Nobody Likes You* for additional usage.

- - - - - - - - - - - *fold* - - - - - - - - - -

Definition: to mock or ridicule someone loudly

Hint in Cursive:

Nabonidus loved to ▓▓▓▓▓▓ *at his sister whenever their mom sent her to time-out.*

cut

cut

cut

Pull top of page toward you, folding across the line below.

- - - - - - - - - - - fold - - - - - - - - - - -

Interact

Example:
In order to type his essay, Hegesippus must **interact** with the computer keyboard.

See p. 20 of *SHUT UP! Nobody Likes You* for additional usage.

- - - - - - - - - - - *fold* - - - - - - - - - -

(Cryptic Composition Card back)

Definition: communicate or engage with others

Hint in Cursive:

In order to type his essay, Hegesippus must _____ with the computer keyboard.

Pull top of page toward you, folding across the line below.

- - - - - - - - - - - - *fold* - - - - - - - - - - -

Tumultuous

Example:
Despite a **tumultuous** start, Lycomedes finished third grade with the highest marks in his class.

See p. 21 of *SHUT UP! Nobody Likes You* for additional usage.
- - - - - - - - - - - fold - - - - - - - - - - -
(Cryptic Composition Card back)

Definition: full of noise, excitement, or confusion

Hint in Cursive:

Despite a ▒▒▒▒▒▒▒ start, Lycomedes finished third grade with the highest marks in his class.

Pull top of page toward you, folding across the line below.

- - - - - - - - - - - *fold* - - - - - - - - - -

Contain

Example:
Bardolph's lunchbox doesn't **contain** an apple or a sandwich today.

See p. 22 of *SHUT UP! Nobody Likes You* for additional usage.

- - - - - - - - - - - - *fold* - - - - - - - - - -

Definition: hold or include something within specified limits

Hint in Cursive:

Bardolph's lunchbox doesn't ▓▓▓▓▓▓ an apple or a sandwich today.

Pull top of page toward you, folding across the line below.

- - - - - - - - - - - *fold* - - - - - - - - - - -

(Cryptic Composition Card front)

Condescend

Example:
Malvolio's professor refused to **condescend** to him, so he spoke to him respectfully.

See p. 22 of *SHUT UP! Nobody Likes You* for additional usage.
- - - - - - - - - - - *fold* - - - - - - - - - - -
(Cryptic Composition Card back)

Definition: to show feelings of superiority; to patronize

Hint in Cursive:

Malvolio's professor refused to   to him, so he spoke to him respectfully.

Pull top of page toward you, folding across the line below.

- - - - - - - - - - - - *fold* - - - - - - - - - - -

Emphatic

Example:

Meliora's mother was **emphatic** about the importance of eating broccoli.

See p. 22 of *SHUT UP! Nobody Likes You* for additional usage.

- - - - - - - - - - - *fold* - - - - - - - - - -

Definition: expressed with emphasis; forceful and clear

Hint in Cursive:

Meliora's mother was ▓▓▓▓▓ about the importance of eating broccoli .

Pull top of page toward you, folding across the line below.

- - - - - - - - - - - *fold* - - - - - - - - - -

Foyer

Example:
Guests gathered in the elegant **foyer** before entering the ballroom.

See p. 22 of *SHUT UP! Nobody Likes You* for additional usage.

- - - - - - - - - - - *fold* - - - - - - - - - -

(Cryptic Composition Card back)

Definition: a lobby or entrance hall in a building

Hint in Cursive:

Guests gathered in the elegant ▓▓▓▓▓ before entering the ballroom.

cut

177

Pull top of page toward you, folding across the line below.

- - - - - - - - - - - *fold* - - - - - - - - - -

Spacious

Example:
The conference hall was **spacious** enough to host a large audience.

See p. 23 of *SHUT UP! Nobody Likes You* for additional usage.
- - - - - - - - - - - *fold* - - - - - - - - - -
(Cryptic Composition Card back)

Definition: having a lot of space; roomy

Hint in Cursive:

The conference hall was ▬▬▬▬ enough to host a large audience.

179

Pull top of page toward you, folding across the line below.

- - - - - - - - - - - *fold* - - - - - - - - - -

Dread

Example:

As the hurricane approached, the dark clouds in the sky brought a feeling of **dread.**

See p. 23 of *SHUT UP! Nobody Likes You* for additional usage.

- - - - - - - - - - - *fold* - - - - - - - - - - -

Definition: anticipate with great fear or apprehension

Hint in Cursive:

As the hurricane approached, the dark clouds in the sky brought a feeling of _____.

cut

Pull top of page toward you, folding across the line below.

- - - - - - - - - - - *fold* - - - - - - - - - -

Elite

Example:
The **elite** group of scientists discovered a new species.

See p. 24 of *SHUT UP! Nobody Likes You* for additional usage.

- - - - - - - - - - - - fold - - - - - - - - - -

Definition: a select group that is superior in terms of ability or qualities

Hint in Cursive:

The ▓▓▓▓▓▓▓ group of scientists discovered a new species.

Pull top of page toward you, folding across the line below.

- - - - - - - - - - - *fold* - - - - - - - - - -

Affluent

Example:
The neighborhood was known for its **affluent** residents and luxurious homes.

See p. 24 of *SHUT UP! Nobody Likes You* for additional usage.

- - - - - - - - - - - *fold* - - - - - - - - - -

Definition: wealthy, having an abundance of resources

Hint in Cursive:

The neighborhood was known for its _____ residents and luxurious homes.

Pull top of page toward you, folding across the line below.

- - - - - - - - - - - *fold* - - - - - - - - - -

Avid

Example:

As an **avid** reader, Cormac's favorite hobby is reading.

See p. 24 of *SHUT UP! Nobody Likes You* for additional usage.

- - - - - - - - - - - *fold* - - - - - - - - - -

Definition: showing fierce interest or enthusiasm

Hint in Cursive:

As an ▓▓▓▓▓▓▓▓ reader, Cormac's favorite hobby is reading.

Pull top of page toward you, folding across the line below.

- - - - - - - - - - - *fold* - - - - - - - - - -

Crave

Example:
After a long run in the summer heat, Amabel and her mom **crave** a cold drink of water.

See p. 25 of *SHUT UP! Nobody Likes You* for additional usage.

- - - - - - - - - - - fold - - - - - - - - - -

Definition: to have an intense desire for something

Hint in Cursive:

After a long run in the summer heat, Amabel and her mom _____ a cold drink of water.

Pull top of page toward you, folding across the line below.

- - - - - - - - - - - *fold* - - - - - - - - - -

(Cryptic Composition Card front)

Antics

Example:
Ragnar's funny **antics** entertained the classroom.

See p. 25 of *SHUT UP! Nobody Likes You* for additional usage.

- - - - - - - - - - - - *fold* - - - - - - - - - - - -

(Cryptic Composition Card back)

Definition: playful or silly actions intended to entertain

Hint in Cursive:

Ragnar's funny
entertained the classroom.

cut

Pull top of page toward you, folding across the line below.

- - - - - - - - - - - *fold* - - - - - - - - - -

Reprimand

Example:
Theobald received a **reprimand** from the teacher when he arrived ten minutes late to class.

See p. 25 of *SHUT UP! Nobody Likes You* for additional usage.
- - - - - - - - - - - *fold* - - - - - - - - - -
(Cryptic Composition Card back)

Definition: express sharp disapproval or criticism of someone's actions

Hint in Cursive:

Theobald received a _____
from the teacher when he arrived ten minutes late to class.

Pull top of page toward you, folding across the line below.

- - - - - - - - - - - - *fold* - - - - - - - - - - -

Denial

Example:
Facing a problem is healthier than living in **denial.**

See p. 27 of *SHUT UP! Nobody Likes You* for additional usage.

- - - - - - - - - - - - *fold* - - - - - - - - - - -

Definition: refusal to accept the truth or reality of something

Hint in Cursive:

Facing a problem is healthier than living in ▨▨▨▨▨▨▨ .

Pull top of page toward you, folding across the line below.

- - - - - - - - - - - - *fold* - - - - - - - - - - -

Distraught

Example:
When his mother refused to take him to the toy store,
Gaspar was **distraught**.

See p. 27 of *SHUT UP! Nobody Likes You* for additional
usage.

- - - - - - - - - - - *fold* - - - - - - - - - - -

(Cryptic Composition Card back)

Definition: extremely upset or agitated

Hint in Cursive:

*When his mother refused to
take him to the toy store,
Gaspar was _____ .*

197

Pull top of page toward you, folding across the line below.

- - - - - - - - - - - *fold* - - - - - - - - - -

Mortified

Example:

Emmeline was **mortified** when her cell phone went off loudly during the church service.

See p. 28 of *SHUT UP! Nobody Likes You* for additional usage.

- - - - - - - - - - - *fold* - - - - - - - - - -

(Cryptic Composition Card back)

Definition: deeply embarrassed or humiliated

Hint in Cursive:

Emmeline was ▓▓▓▓▓ when her cell phone went off loudly during the church service.

Pull top of page toward you, folding across the line below.

- - - - - - - - - - - fold - - - - - - - - - - -

Distinguished

Example:

As a **distinguished** athlete, Jorund broke several world records.

See p. 29 of *SHUT UP! Nobody Likes You* for additional usage.

- - - - - - - - - - - - - fold - - - - - - - - - -

Definition: recognized and respected for excellence and achievements

Hint in Cursive:

As a ▬▬▬▬▬ athlete, Jorund broke several world records.

Pull top of page toward you, folding across the line below.

- - - - - - - - - - - *fold* - - - - - - - - - -

(Cryptic Composition Card front)

Festivity

Example:
Delicious treats and meals are part of the holiday **festivity.**

See p. 29 of *SHUT UP! Nobody Likes You* for additional usage.

- - - - - - - - - - - - *fold* - - - - - - - - - - - -

(Cryptic Composition Card back)

Definition: the celebration of a festival or event with joy and merriment

Hint in Cursive:

Delicious treats and meals are part of the holiday ________.

cut

Pull top of page toward you, folding across the line below.

- - - - - - - - - - - *fold* - - - - - - - - - -

Mandate

Example:
The school's dress code doesn't **mandate** that all
students must wear a blazer.

See p. 29 of *SHUT UP! Nobody Likes You* for additional
usage.

- - - - - - - - - - - *fold* - - - - - - - - - - -

Definition: an official order or command

Hint in Cursive:

The school's dress code doesn't ▓▓▓▓▓▓ that all students must wear a blazer.

Pull top of page toward you, folding across the line below.

- - - - - - - - - - - - fold - - - - - - - - - - - -

(Cryptic Composition Card front)

Detest

Example:
Osbert and Arlo **detest** spinach and complain when their mother forces them to eat it.

See p. 29 of *SHUT UP! Nobody Likes You* for additional usage.

- - - - - - - - - - - - *fold* - - - - - - - - - - - -

(Cryptic Composition Card back)

Definition: intensely dislike or loathe

Hint in Cursive:

Osbert and Arlo
spinach and complain when their
mother forces them to eat it.

cut

cut

cut

Pull top of page toward you, folding across the line below.

- - - - - - - - - - - - *fold* - - - - - - - - - - -

Longing

Example:
As Ottilie traveled to the other side of the world, she began **longing** for home.

See p. 29 of *SHUT UP! Nobody Likes You* for additional usage.

- - - - - - - - - - - *fold* - - - - - - - - - -

Definition: a strong, persistent desire or yearning

Hint in Cursive:

As Ottilie traveled to the other side of the world, she began _____ for home.

Pull top of page toward you, folding across the line below.

- - - - - - - - - - - - *fold* - - - - - - - - - - -

Nimble

Example:
The pianist's **nimble** fingers worked quickly up and
down the keyboard.

See p. 30 of *SHUT UP! Nobody Likes You* for additional
usage.

- - - - - - - - - - - - fold - - - - - - - - - - -

(Cryptic Composition Card back)

Definition: quick and light in movement or action

Hint in Cursive:

*The pianist's ▒▒▒▒▒▒▒▒ fingers
worked quickly up and down the
keyboard!*

cut

Pull top of page toward you, folding across the line below.

- - - - - - - - - - - - *fold* - - - - - - - - - - - -

Accustomed

Example:
Growing up in a buy city, Ismenia was **accustomed** to the constant noise.

See p. 30 of *SHUT UP! Nobody Likes You* for additional usage.

- - - - - - - - - - - - - *fold* - - - - - - - - - -

Definition: familiar with or used to something

Hint in Cursive:

Growing up in a busy city, Ismenia was ▨▨▨▨▨ to the constant noise .

cut

Pull top of page toward you, folding across the line below.

- - - - - - - - - - - - *fold* - - - - - - - - - - -

(Cryptic Composition Card front)

Integrate

Example:
A buddy system is a great way to **integrate** new students into the school.

See p. 30 of *SHUT UP! Nobody Likes You* for additional usage.

\- - - - - - - - - - - - *fold* - - - - - - - - - - - -

(Cryptic Composition Card back)

Definition: to combine or bring together into a unified whole

Hint in Cursive:

A buddy system is a great
way to ________ new
students into the school.

cut

Pull top of page toward you, folding across the line below.

- - - - - - - - - - - - *fold* - - - - - - - - - - -

Disorient

Example:
Being blindfolded can **disorient** you and increase your
risk of stumbling.

See p. 31 of *SHUT UP! Nobody Likes You* for additional
usage.
- - - - - - - - - - - - - *fold* - - - - - - - - - -

Definition: cause someone to lose their sense of
direction or understanding

Hint in Cursive:

Being blindfolded can ▓▓▓▓▓▓▓▓ you and increase your risk of stumbling.

Pull top of page toward you, folding across the line below.

- - - - - - - - - - - - - *fold* - - - - - - - - - - - -

Morale

Example:
Romilly's motivational speech significantly improved her team's **morale.**

See p. 31 of *SHUT UP! Nobody Likes You* for additional usage.

- - - - - - - - - - - - *fold* - - - - - - - - - -

(Cryptic Composition Card back)

Definition: the confidence, enthusiasm, and discipline of a person or group

Hint in Cursive:

Romilly's motivational speech significantly improved her team's ▬▬▬▬ .

Pull top of page toward you, folding across the line below.

- - - - - - - - - - - *fold* - - - - - - - - - -

Blatant

Example:
Cuthbert's **blatant** cheating on the examination was
caught on camera.

See p. 31 of *SHUT UP! Nobody Likes You* for additional
usage.

- - - - - - - - - - - *fold* - - - - - - - - - -

(Cryptic Composition Card back)

Definition: very obvious and intentional, often
offensive

Hint in Cursive:

*Cuthbert's ▓▓▓▓▓▓▓ cheating
on the examination was caught
on camera.*

cut

cut

cut

Pull top of page toward you, folding across the line below.

- - - - - - - - - - - - *fold* - - - - - - - - - - -

Composure

Example:
Box breathing can help a person regain **composure** during stressful situations.

See p. 31 of *SHUT UP! Nobody Likes You* for additional usage.
- - - - - - - - - - - *fold* - - - - - - - - - -
(Cryptic Composition Card back)

Definition: the state of being calm and collected

Hint in Cursive:

Box breathing can help a person regain ▓▓▓▓▓▓ during stressful situations.

Pull top of page toward you, folding across the line below.

- - - - - - - - - - - - *fold* - - - - - - - - - - -

Coincidence

Example:
Meeting an old friend in a foreign land is a
remarkable **coincidence.**

See p. 31 of *SHUT UP! Nobody Likes You* for additional
usage.
- - - - - - - - - - - *fold* - - - - - - - - - -
(Cryptic Composition Card back)

Definition: a remarkable concurrence of events without
apparent cause

Hint in Cursive:

Meeting an old friend in
a foreign land is a remarkable
_____ .

Pull top of page toward you, folding across the line below.

- - - - - - - - - - - *fold* - - - - - - - - - -

Consult

Example:
Boethius refused to **consult** his parents before leaving the house at night.

See p. 31 of *SHUT UP! Nobody Likes You* for additional usage.
- - - - - - - - - - - *fold* - - - - - - - - - -
(Cryptic Composition Card back)

Definition: to seek information or advice from someone

Hint in Cursive:

Boethius refused to ▒▒▒▒▒▒▒
his parents before leaving the
house at night.

227

Pull top of page toward you, folding across the line below.

- - - - - - - - - - - *fold* - - - - - - - - - -

(Cryptic Composition Card front)

Derogatory

Example:
Gundred used **derogatory** language and was promptly kicked out of the dining hall.

cut

\- - - - - - - - - - - - - *fold* - - - - - - - - - - - - -

(Cryptic Composition Card back)

Definition: expressive of a low opinion; detracting from the character or standing of something

Hint in Cursive:

Gundred used ______ language and was promptly kicked out of the dining hall.

cut

cut

Pull top of page toward you, folding across the line below.

- - - - - - - - - - - *fold* - - - - - - - - - -

Lampoon

Example:

Hadrian had the assembly in an uproar as he tried to **lampoon** silly habits of human beings.

- - - - - - - - - - - - fold - - - - - - - - - - -

Definition: to mock or ridicule someone or something, especially through humor or satire

Hint in Cursive:

Hadrian had the assembly in uproar as he tried to _____ silly habits of human beings.

Pull top of page toward you, folding across the line below.

- - - - - - - - - - - *fold* - - - - - - - - - - -

Cryptic Writing

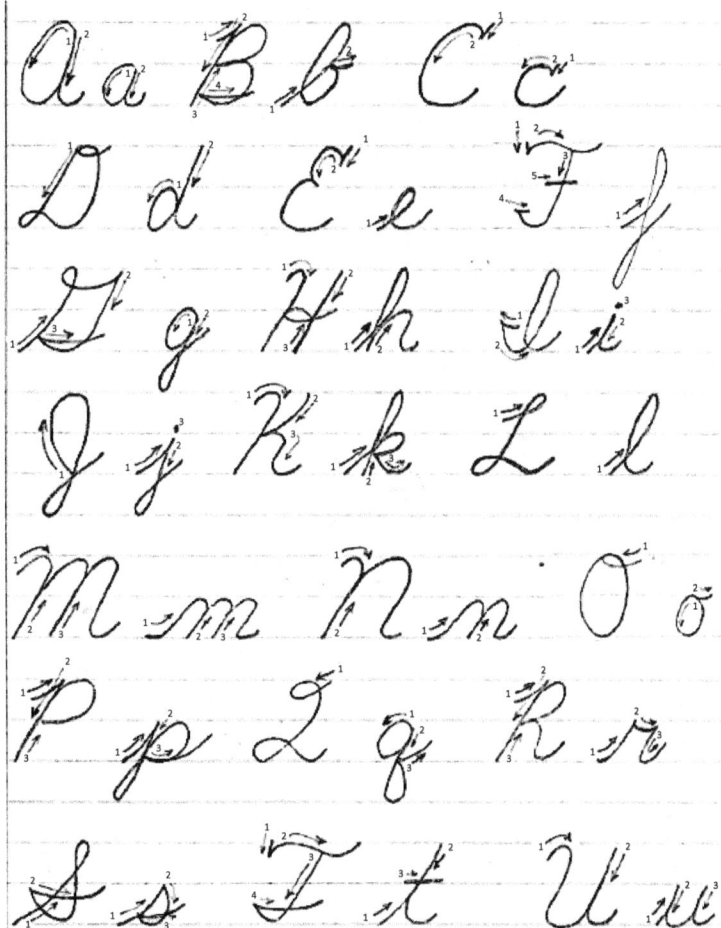

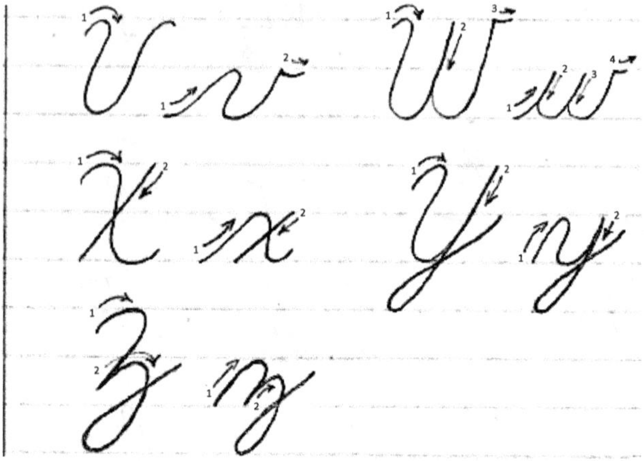

1
2
1
1
2
3
2
4
3
1
1
2
1
2
1
2
1
2
1
2
1
2

In the lines provided, copy the cursive sentences:

Calculus only appears **cryptic** until you start
practicing problems.

Calculus only appears cryptic
until you start practicing
problems.

_____

_____

_____

_____

_____

_____

_____

Gautfred consumed dessert in **excess** and developed a
tummy ache.

Gautfred consumed dessert in
excess and developed a
tummy ache.

Florian like to **affix** skateboard stickers to the front
door of his home for decoration.

Florian likes to affix *skateboard stickers to the front door of his home.*

Before singing on stage, Norbert issued a **disclaimer** to the audience about the strobe lights he used in his act.

Before singing on stage, Norbert issued a disclaimer to the audience about the strobe lights he used in his act.

In **academia,** people work together to learn and share
knowledge.

*In academia, people work
together to learn and share
knowledge.*

_____

_____

_____

_____

_____

_____

Olaf grew annoyed when the restaurant served him a
measly portion of meat.

Olaf grew annoyed when the
restaurant served him a
measly portion of meat.

Malena wants to **leverage** her computer skills to teach her grandparents how to use macros.

Malena wants to leverage *her computer skills to teach her grandparents how to use macros.*

_____

_____

_____

_____

_____

_____

Torkel watched in **utter** disbelief as the chef served him a child-sized portion of stew.

Torkel watched in utter disbelief as the chef served him a child-sized portion of stew.

Fritigern's favorite **facet** of math is trigonometry.

Fritigern's favorite facet *of math is trigonometry.*

Whenever their mother refuses to buy candy, Gildas and Catrin **enumerate** the reasons they deserve a treat.

Whenever their mother refuses to buy candy, Gildas and Catrin **enumerate** *the reasons they deserve a treat.*

Ever the **savvy** shopper, Ambrosius waited for a sale before purchasing his lacrosse helmet.

Ever the savvy *shopper, Ambrosius waited for a sale before purchasing his lacrosse helmet.*

Intrigued by a paper she read on rocket science,
Rosamund began studying physics and chemistry.

Intrigued by a paper she read on rocket science, Rosamund began studying physics and chemistry.

After annoying his mother, Hengist needed an excellent
sales **pitch** to convince her to lend him $25.

After annoying his mother, Hengist
needed an excellent sales pitch
to convince her to lend him $25.

The teacher offered Vetranio extra credit to **articulate**
his point of view during class.

The teacher offered Vetranio extra
credit to articulate his point of
view during class.

In line for Chinese food, Nennius filled up on free
beef samples provided to each **patron**.

In line for Chinese food, Nennius
filled up on free beef samples
provided to each **patron** .

I wore mismatched gym shoes to the dance, and my
friends didn't hesitate to **lambaste** me for the silly
decision.

I wore mismatched gym shoes
to the dance, and my friends didn't
hesitate to **lambaste** me for the
silly decision.

_____

_____

_____

_____

_____

_____

_____

I fought to **stifle** my laughs as Tilghman made silly faces at me during the calculus examination.

I fought to stifle my laughs as Tilghman made silly faces at me during the calculus examination.

Cenwald and his sisters displayed **primitive** behavior by
yelling and running through the mall.

Cenwald and his sisters displayed
primitive behavior by yelling
and running through the mall.

_____

_____

_____

_____

_____

_____

_____

The server would **exasperate** Leodegar anytime she
brought a dish that didn't include the amount of meat
he paid for.

The server would exasperate
Leodegar anytime she brought a dish
that didn't include the amount of
meat he paid for.

Vittorio couldn't **persuade** his calculus teacher to allow an extra twenty minutes on the test.

Vittorio couldn't persuade his calculus teacher to allow an extra twenty minutes on the test.

After winning the tournament, the **elated** baseball team cheered and jumped for joy.

After winning the tournament, the elated baseball team cheered and jumped for joy.

People often **degrade** criminal offenders who have been
released from prison.

People often degrade *criminal
offenders who have been released from
prison.*

The outcome of Beltran's academic **neglect** was a poor grade on the quiz.

The outcome of Beltran's academic neglect was a poor grade on the quiz.

Petronilla worked with her family members to
orchestrate Mom's surprise birthday party.

Petronilla worked with her family members to orchestrate Mom's surprise birthday party.

When Thrasamund and his sister trek through the dense
forest, they often **encounter** brown bears.

When, Thrasamund and his sister trek through the dense forest, they often **encounter** *brown bears.*

His mother's insistence that he redo his sloppy
handwriting caused Benvolio to **resent** her all morning.

His mother's insistence that he redo
his sloppy handwriting caused
Benvolio to **resent** her all
morning.

After receiving socks for Christmas instead of the skateboard he was promised, Baldwin gave a **lukewarm** "thank you" to his aunt.

After receiving socks for Christmas instead of the skateboard he was promised, Baldwin gave a lukewarm "thank you" to his aunt.

Refusing a handshake is a **slight** that usually upsets
people.

Refusing a handshake is a `slight`
that usually upsets people.

After being caught in a lie, Leofric became **hostile** and
yelled at the reporter.

After being caught in a lie, Leofrick became hostile *and yelled at the reporter.*

Sigebert held his grandmother's hand as she walked down
the icy walkway because she was **prone** to falling
without her cane.

Sigebert held his grandmother's hand as she walked down the icy walkway because she was prone *to falling without her cane.*

The day after she left for the beach, Volkmar and his friends used his aunt's castle to host **lavish** dinner parties.

The day after she left for the beach, Volkmar and his friends used his aunt's castle to host lavish dinner parties.

Atop the mountain, Adhemar observed the **sprawling**
woodlands and beautiful, fruited plains.

Atop the mountain, Adhemar observed the sprawling *woodlands and beautiful fruited plains.*

After an intense gym class, waiting in line for the
water fountain was an **excruciating** test of patience for
Ingjald.

After an intense gym class, waiting
in line for the water fountain
was an excruciating test of
patience for Ingjald.

Archibald and his brother **shun** mashed potatoes anytime
their father serves meatloaf.

Archibald and his brother shun *mashed potatoes anytime their father serves meatloaf.*

_____

_____

_____

_____

_____

_____

_____

Diggory enjoys candy, but he starts to **grouse** when it's time to eat green beans.

Diggory enjoys candy, but he starts to **grouse** when it's time to eat green beans.

After earning a C on her mid-term, Desideria was
relentless in her studies, and she fought her way back
to an A.

After earning a C on her mid-term,
Desideria was relentless in her
studies, and she fought her way back
to an A.

Balthasar was **reluctant** to paint his cousin's castle for free.

Balthasar was reluctant to paint his cousin's castle for free.

Eadwig mocked his teacher, showing **overt** disrespect.

Eadwig mocked his teacher, showing overt disrespect.

The neighborhood threw an "adults only" party to
exclude all children.

The neighborhood threw an "adults only" party to exclude *all children.*

After Fulbert accidentally dropped his cup on his mother's white couch, she could never remove the grape-juice **taint**.

After Fulbert accidentally dropped his cup on his mother's white couch, she could never remove the grape-juice **taint** .

_____

_____

_____

_____

_____

_____

_____

Every day after school, Thaddeus and his friends **mount** their skateboards and fly down the street.

Every day after school, Thaddeus and his friends **mount** *their skateboards and fly down the street.*

When skydiving for the first time, many are too
petrified to jump from the plane.

When skydiving for the first time, many are too petrified *to jump from the plane.*

With arms **akimbo**, Elfrida's annoyed teacher waited for
the noisy class to quiet down.

With arms akimbo *,*
Elfrida's annoyed teacher waited
for the noisy class to quiet
down.

After intentionally kicking the basketball into the
bleachers, Millicent observed a **stern** look on her
coach's face.

After intentionally kicking the basketball into the bleachers, Millicent observed a **stern** *look on her coach's face.*

Whenever Laodocus grew tired, his angry drill sergeant
would **bellow** commands in his face.

*Whenever Laodocus grew tired, his
angry drill sergeant would* **bellow**
commands in his face.

_____

_____

_____

_____

_____

_____

_____

Astrid was **dumbfounded** when her server delivered a
charred ribeye after she requested rare.

Astrid was dumbfounded when.
her server delivered a charred ribeye
after she requested rare.

With a heart full of **malice,** the villain plotted to rob
retirement home.

With a heart full of ⬚malice⬚,
the villain plotted to rob
retirement homes.

_____

_____

_____

_____

_____

_____

_____

Erasmus sought help from his teacher because the
complicated instructions **bewilder** everyone who tries to
make sense of them.

Erasmus sought help from his teacher
because the complicated instructions
bewilder everyone who tries
to make sense of them.

Margery loved to **recline** in her beach chair,
outstretching her feet and taking a deep breath of
satisfaction.

Margery loved to recline *in her
beach chair, outstretching her feet
and taking a deep breath of
satisfaction.*

As the referee declared the winner of the tournament,
the losing team glared at their opponents in **spite.**

As the referee declared the
winner of the tournament, the
losing team glared at their
opponents in   spite   .

Rain had caused the abandoned building to **deteriorate** so badly that the floors were hazardous.

Rain had caused the abandoned building to deteriorate *so badly that the floors were hazardous.*

_____

_____

_____

_____

_____

_____

_____

Having never seen snow before, the African exchange student stopped to **marvel** at the snowman standing before him.

Having never seen snow before, the African exchange student stopped to marvel at the snowman standing before him.

Physically exhausted, Oriana relied on her **willpower** to finish the marathon.

Physically exhausted, Oriana relied on her willpower to finish the marathon.

_____

_____

_____

_____

_____

_____

_____

During a group project, it's important to **acknowledge**
the hard work and contributions of other team members.

During a group project it's important
to acknowledge the hard work
and contributions of other team
members.

We were **awestruck** by the beauty of the magnificent
sunset.

We were awestruck by the
beauty of the magnificent
sunset.

As Arnaud prepared to **venture** into the deadly Amazon
rainforest, he gathered supplies.

As Arnaud prepared to venture
into the deadly Amazon rainforest,
he gathered supplies.

The lacrosse coach was **livid** with Hrothgar's lazy
performance during the game.

The lacrosse coach was `livid`
with Hrothgar's lazy performance
during the game.

Isidore and his sisters **defy** bedtime rules by playing
with electronics under the covers.

Isidore and his sisters **defy**
bedtime rules by playing with
electronics under the covers.

_____

_____

_____

_____

_____

_____

Using foul language to insult others can **alienate** you from your peers.

Using foul language to insult others can alienate you from your peers.

Each student has a **distinct** personality and may have different hobbies too.

Each student has a distinct *personality and may have different hobbies too.*

The skilled pilot was able to **maneuver** the aircraft through the hurricane.

The skilled pilot was able to maneuver *the aircraft through the hurricane.*

The house was located at the end of a quiet **cul-de-sac,**
providing a peaceful living environment.

The house was located at
the end of a quiet cul-de-sac,
providing a peaceful living
environment.

Arabella's studies so **engross** her that she often
doesn't care to go out and play.

Arabella's studies so ██████ engross ██████
her that she often doesn't care to
go out and play.

Patroclus and his friends routinely **engage** in science
experiments at school.

Patroclus and his friends routinely
engage in science
experiments at school.

Gullveig only needed a few seconds to **transfer** her
textbooks from her backpack to the desk.

Gullveig only needed a few seconds to **transfer** *her textbooks from her backpack to the desk.*

Polonius added an **inordinate** amount of spice to the stew, making it extremely hot.

Polonius added an inordinate amount of spice to the stew, making it extremely hot.

Choosing not to **boast** about her skills, Ophelia let her
performance speak for itself.

Choosing not to boast
about her skills, Ophelia let
her performance speak for
itself.

The vocabulary flashcards will **afford** Bernardo the opportunity to learn cool, funny words.

The vocabulary flashcards will afford Bernardo the opportunity to learn cool, funny words.

Clovis was **dedicated** to perfecting the piano piece, and he practiced hours each day.

Clovis was dedicated to perfecting the piano piece, and he practiced hours each day.

Heraclitus made **considerable** progress when he improved
his grade from 70% to 95%.

Heraclitus made considerable
progress when he improved his grade
from 70% to 95%!

_____

_____

_____

_____

_____

_____

_____

Edmund played happily in the living room, his toys
strewn about.

Edmund played happily in
the living room, his toys
strewn about.

Before returning to school for the spring semester,
Pericles and his friends made plans to **reconvene** in the
dining hall.

Before returning to school for the
spring semester, Pericles and his
friends made plans to reconvene
in the dining hall.

The rival teams displayed **animosity** by taunting and
fighting each other during the game.

The rival teams displayed
animosity by taunting and
fighting each other during
the game.

Tarquin's silly idea about building a time machine caused his father to **scoff**.

Tarquin's silly idea about building a time machine caused his father to scoff.

Nabonidus loved to **jeer** at his sister whenever their mom sent her to time-out.

Nabonidus loved to ░░░░ jeer ░░░░ at his sister whenever their mom sent her to time-out.

In order to type his essay, Hegesippus must **interact**
with the computer keyboard.

In order to type his essay,
Hegesippus must interact
with the computer keyboard.

Despite a **tumultuous** start, Lycomedes finished third
grade with the highest marks in his class.

Despite a tumultuous *start,*
Lycomedes finished third grade
with the highest marks in his
class.

Bardolph's lunchbox doesn't **contain** an apple or a
sandwich today.

Bardolph's lunchbox, doesn't
contain an apple or a
sandwich today.

Malvolio's professor refused to **condescend** to him, so
he spoke to him respectfully.

Malvolio's professor refused to condescend to him, so he spoke to him respectfully.

_____

_____

_____

_____

_____

_____

Meliora's mother was **emphatic** about the importance of eating broccoli.

Meliora's mother was emphatic *about the importance of eating broccoli .*

_____

_____

_____

_____

_____

_____

_____

Guests gathered in the elegant **foyer** before entering
the ballroom.

Guests gathered in the elegant
foyer before entering the
ballroom.

The conference hall was **spacious** enough to host a large audience.

The conference hall was spacious enough to host a large audience.

As the hurricane approached, the dark clouds in the sky
brought a feeling of **dread**.

As the hurricane approached, the dark clouds in the sky brought a feeling of dread *.*

The **elite** group of scientists discovered a new species.

The   elite   group of scientists
discovered a new species.

The neighborhood was known for its **affluent** residents and luxurious homes.

The neighborhood was known for its affluent residents and luxurious homes.

As an **avid** reader, Cormac's favorite hobby is reading.

As an ~~avid~~ reader, Cormac's favorite hobby is reading.

_____

_____

_____

_____

_____

_____

_____

After a long run in the summer heat, Amabel and her mom **crave** a cold drink of water.

After a long run in the summer heat, Amabel and her mom crave a cold drink of water.

Ragnar's funny **antics** entertained the classroom.

Ragnar's funny antics *entertained the classroom.*

Theobald received a **reprimand** from the teacher when he arrived ten minutes late to class.

Theobald received a reprimand from the teacher when he arrived ten minutes late to class.

_____

_____

_____

_____

_____

_____

_____

Facing a problem is healthier than living in **denial.**

Facing a problem is healthier than living in denial .

_____

_____

_____

_____

_____

_____

_____

When his mother refused to take him to the toy store,
Gaspar was **distraught**.

When his mother refused to
take him to the toy store,
Gaspar was ____distraught____.

Emmeline was **mortified** when her cell phone went off
loudly during the church service.

Emmeline was mortified
when her cell phone went off
loudly during the church
service.

As a **distinguished** athlete, Jorund broke several world
records.

As a distinguished athlete,
Jorund broke several world
records.

Delicious treats and meals are part of the holiday **festivity**.

Delicious treats and meals are part of the holiday festivity .

The school's dress code doesn't **mandate** that all
students must wear a blazer.

The school's dress code doesn't mandate *that all students
must wear a blazer.*

_____

_____

_____

_____

_____

_____

_____

Osbert and Arlo **detest** spinach and complain when their
mother forces them to eat it.

Osbert and Arlo detest
spinach and complain when their
mother forces them to eat it.

As Ottilie traveled to the other side of the world, she
began **longing** for home.

As Ottilie traveled to the
other side of the world, she
began longing for home.

The pianist's **nimble** fingers worked quickly up and down the keyboard.

The pianist's nimble *fingers worked quickly up and down the keyboard.*

Growing up in a busy city, Ismenia was **accustomed** to
the constant noise.

Growing up in a busy city
Ismenia was accustomed to the
constant noise.

A buddy system is a great way to **integrate** new students into the school.

A buddy system is a great way to integrate new students into the school.

Being blindfolded can **disorient** you and increase your
risk of stumbling.

Being blindfolded can disorient *you and increase your risk of stumbling.*

_____

_____

_____

_____

_____

_____

Romilly's motivational speech significantly improved
her team's **morale.**

Romilly's motivational speech
significantly improved her team's
morale.

Cuthbert's **blatant** cheating on the examination was caught on camera.

Cuthbert's blatant cheating on the examination was caught on camera.

Box breathing can help a person regain **composure** during stressful situations.

Box breathing can help a person regain composure during stressful situations.

Meeting an old friend in a foreign city is a remarkable
coincidence.

*Meeting an old friend in
a foreign land is a remarkable
coincidence* .

Boethius refused to **consult** his parents before leaving
the house at night.

Boethius refused to ▨▨▨ consult
his parents before leaving the
house at night.

_____

_____

_____

_____

_____

_____

_____

Gundred used **derogatory** language and was promptly
kicked out of the dining hall.

Gundred used derogatory
language and was promptly
kicked out of the dining
hall.

_____

_____

_____

_____

_____

_____

_____

_____

Hadrian had the assembly in an uproar as he tried to **lampoon** silly habits of human beings.

Hadrian had the assembly in uproar as he tried to lampoon *silly habits of human beings.*

<∏Γ˙□□

ROCKET SCIENCE

Among many things, rocket scientists know all about chemistry. Would you like to be a rocket scientist? Here's your starting point!

Matter

Matter is anything that occupies space and has mass. Examples of matter: people, cotton candy, stones, chemicals, etc.

Nucleus

Made up of protons and neutrons, the nucleus is the center of an atom; contains nearly all mass of atom

Proton

A proton is a subatomic particle that is found inside the nucleus of an atom. It carries a positive electric charge

Neutron

A neutron is a subatomic particle that is found inside the nucleus of an atom. Neutrons are electrically neutral, meaning that they carry no charge

Atom

An atom is the basic unit of matter. It's made up of
a nucleus that contains positively charged protons
as well as uncharged neutrons. Negatively charged
electrons orbit the nucleus

Element

An element is a substance that consists of only one
type of atom. Hydrogen is an element, and so is
oxygen

Electron

An electron is a subatomic particle with a negative
electric charge. It is found orbiting outside the
nucleus of an atom

Molecule

A molecule is a collection of atoms bonded together

Isotope

Two or more types of atoms of a chemical element
with the same atomic number but with different
physical properties

Covalent Bond

A chemical bond created when atoms share electrons

Valence Shell

An atom's outermost shell; houses the valence
electrons

Oxygen Atom

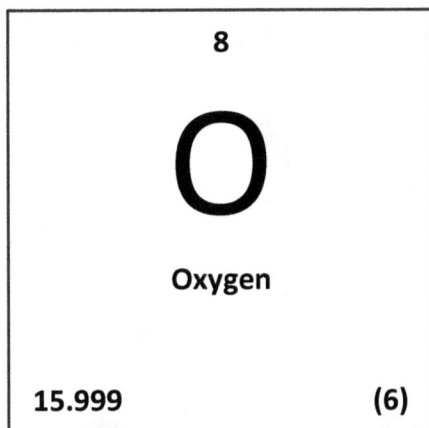

The **atomic number** (8) of an oxygen atom indicates the total number of protons in its nucleus, while its **atomic mass** (15.999amu) represents the average weight of all its protons, neutrons, and electrons. While there are 8 total electrons, (6) **valence electrons** are located in the outermost energy shell of an oxygen atom and determine its chemical behavior.

Note: An oxygen molecule (O_2) is made up of 2 oxygen atoms.

Two Electron Shells Surrounding an Oxygen Atom:
Note: The inner shell contains 2 electrons, while the
outer "valence" shell contains 6 electrons.

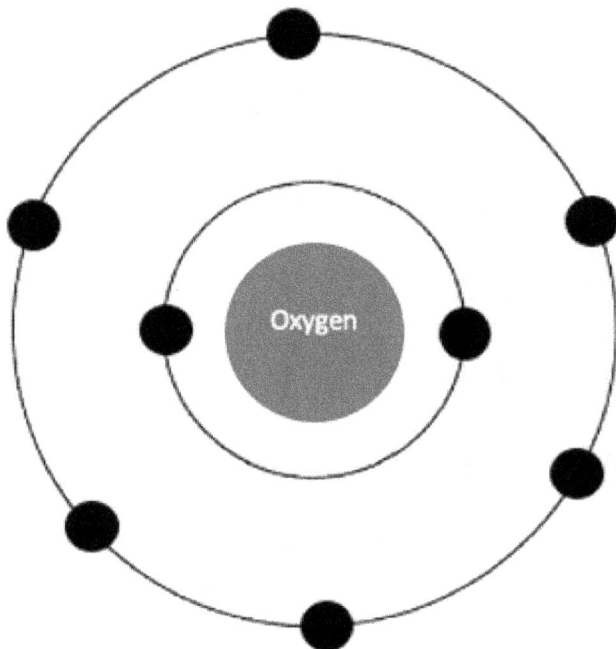

Carbon Atom

```
        6

        C

      Carbon

12.011              (4)
```

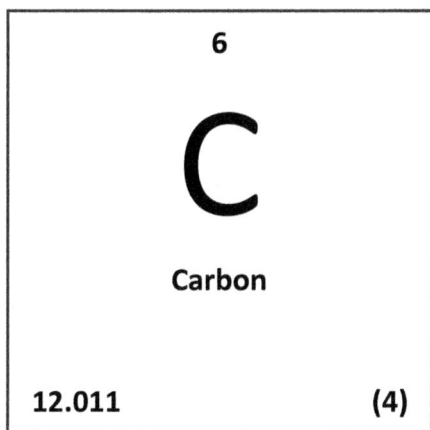

The **atomic number** (6) of a carbon atom indicates the
total number of protons in its nucleus, while its
atomic mass (12.011amu) represents the average weight
of all its protons, neutrons, and electrons. While
there are (6) total electrons, (4) **valence electrons**
are located in the outermost energy shell of a carbon
atom, and they determine its chemical behavior.

Two Electron Shells Surrounding a Carbon Atom:

Note: The inner shell contains 2 electrons, while the outer "valence" shell contains 4 electrons.

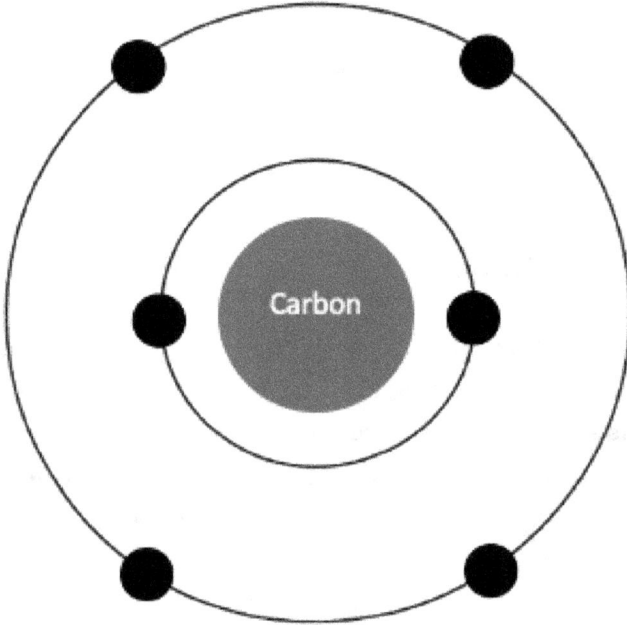

Hydrogen Atom

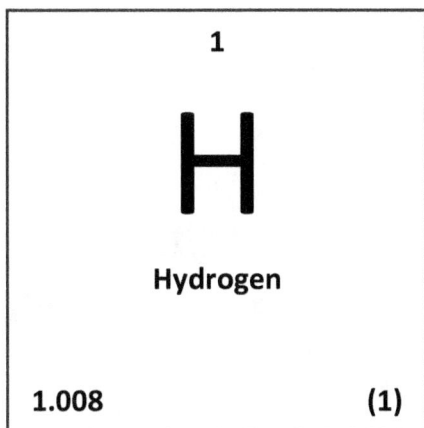

1
H
Hydrogen
1.008   **(1)**

The **atomic number** (1) of a hydrogen atom indicates the total number of protons in its nucleus, while its **atomic mass** (1.008amu) represents the average weight of all its protons, neutrons, and electrons. Hydrogen's only electron (1) is considered its **valence electron,** as it's located in the only energy shell of the hydrogen atom. This electron determines hydrogen's chemical behavior.

One Electron Shell Surrounding a Hydrogen Atom:
One shell contains the only electron.

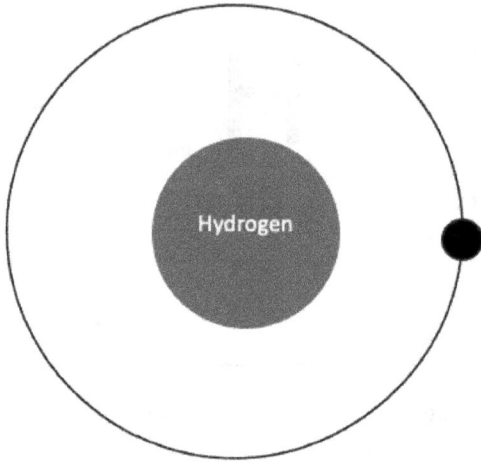

Structure of a Water Molecule

A water molecule is made of two hydrogen atoms and one oxygen atom covalently bonded together.

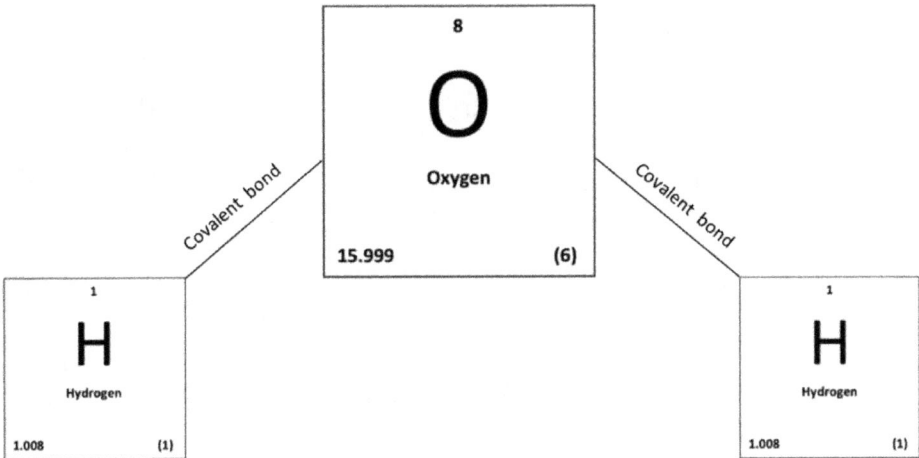

Next Steps:
If you truly want to be a rocket scientist, research the following calculated questions:

- How does a rocket scientist use a periodic table?
- Why are some metals liquid?
- When will a solid turn directly into a gas, and what is this process called?
- What are ionic bonds, and how are they different from metallic bonds?
- How do we predict the behavior of complex molecules and reactions?

CCΛΓ·

AVIATION

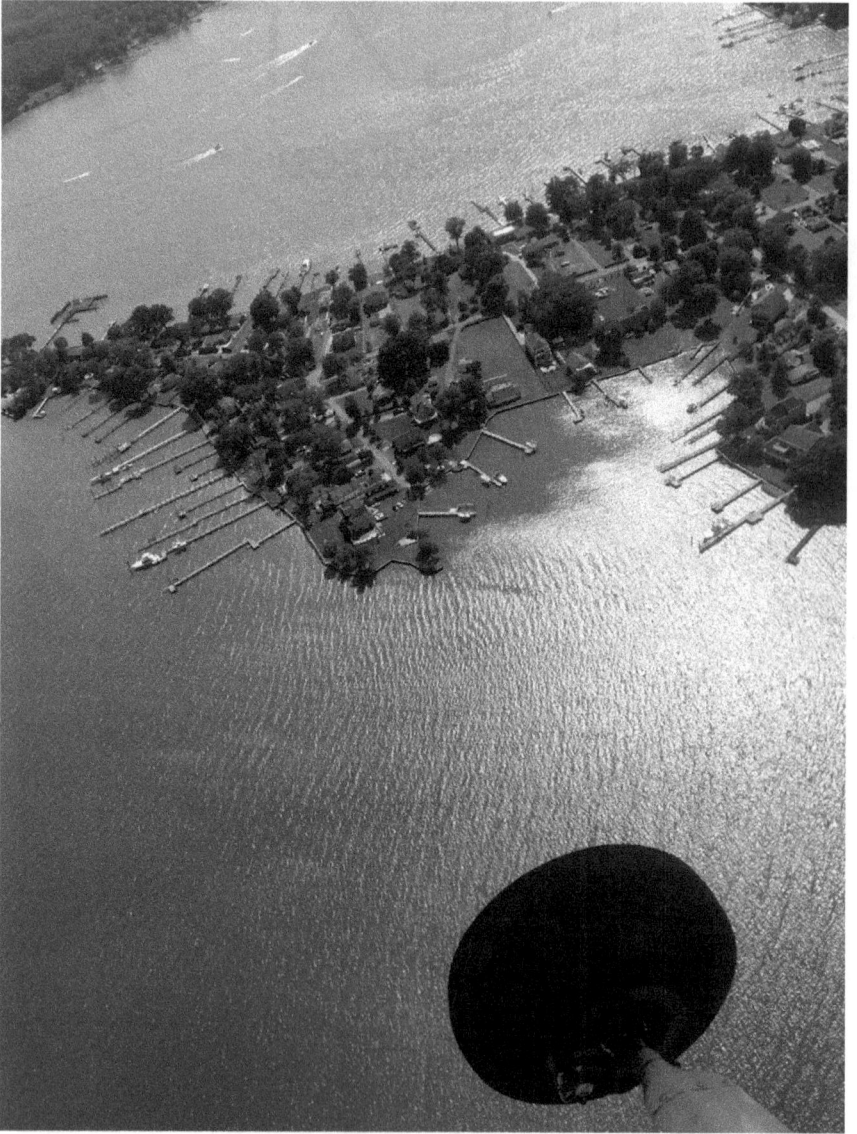

A beautiful day in the sky

Glass cockpit

My brother

Would you like to be a pilot? Here's your starting point!

Military Time vs. Standard Time

Military Time	Standard Time
00:00	12:00 AM
01:00	1:00 AM
02:00	2:00 AM
03:00	3:00 AM
04:00	4:00 AM
05:00	5:00 AM
06:00	6:00 AM
07:00	7:00 AM
08:00	8:00 AM
09:00	9:00 AM
10:00	10:00 AM
11:00	11:00 AM
12:00	12:00 PM
13:00	1:00 PM
14:00	2:00 PM
15:00	3:00 PM
16:00	4:00 PM
17:00	5:00 PM
18:00	6:00 PM
19:00	7:00 PM
20:00	8:00 PM
21:00	9:00 PM
22:00	10:00 PM
23:00	11:00 PM

Pitot Tube

Used for measuring the airspeed of an airplane

The Four Forces of Flight

Lift, weight, thrust, drag

Lift

The aerodynamic force acting perpendicular to the relative wind; produced by the wings, enables an aircraft to counteract the force of gravity and remain airborne

Weight

The gravitational force exerted on an aircraft's mass, acting vertically downward toward the Earth's center; a product of the aircraft's mass and the aircraft's acceleration due to gravity ($9.8m/s^2$)

Thrust

The force generated by an aircraft's propulsion system (i.e., engines or propellers) that propels the aircraft forward through the air; acts in the direction of the aircraft's motion and opposes drag

Drag

The aerodynamic force that opposes an aircraft's direction of flight; minimizing drag is essential for efficient flight performance

The Axes of Control

Roll, pitch, yaw

Roll

Controlled mainly by the ailerons, the rotation of an aircraft (from nose to tail) around its longitudinal axis

Pitch

Controlled mainly by the elevators, the rotation of
an aircraft (from wingtip to wingtip) around its
lateral axis, and perpendicular to its longitudinal
axis

Yaw

Controlled mainly by the rudder, the rotation of an
aircraft around its vertical axis, which extends
vertically through the aircraft's center of gravity

Mach Number

Represents the ratio of the speed of an aircraft to
the speed of sound in the surrounding air; Mach 1 is
the speed of sound, while Mach 2 is twice the speed
of sound

Cut out this page and affix it to a wall in your room.

The Axis of Rotation of an Airplane

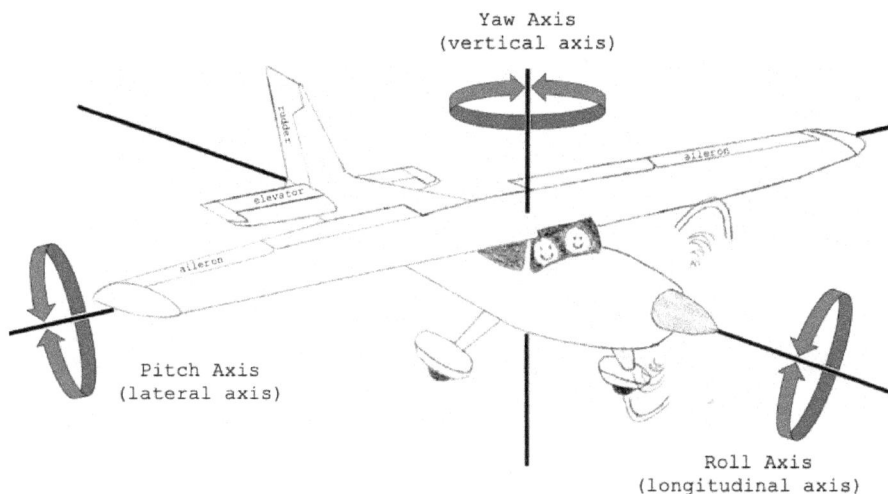

Yaw Axis
(vertical axis)

Pitch Axis
(lateral axis)

Roll Axis
(longitudinal axis)

Next Steps:

If you truly want to be a pilot, research the following calculated questions:

- Relative to sound, how fast is Mach 3?
- What's the purpose of a pre-flight inspection?
- When does a pilot fly with instruments only?
- How do we avoid hot mics?
- As you approach an airport to land the plane, who must you communicate with?
- In the event of catastrophic engine failure, many planes can glide safely to the ground. How does that work?

- In the image below:
  - Color the rudder red
  - Leave the elevators white
  - Color the ailerons blue
  - Give the rest of the plane a color of your choice
  - Label the yaw axis
  - Label the pitch axis
  - Label the roll axis

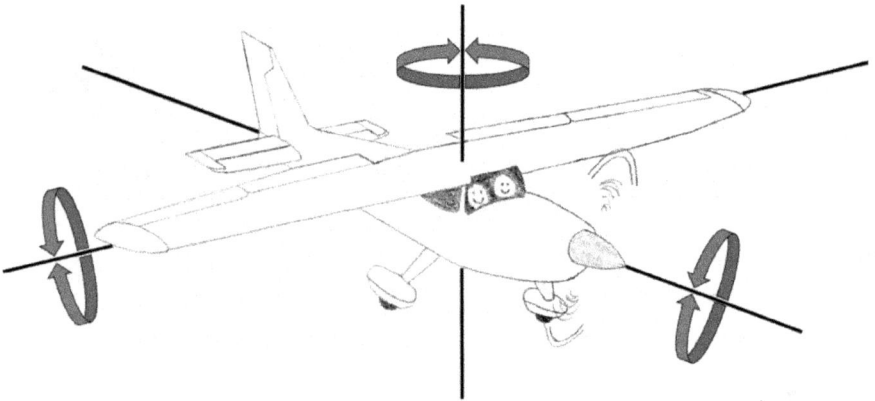

MEDICINE

Doctors save lives every day. Would you like to be a doctor? Here's your starting point!

Research the following topics:

Enzymes

Cellular Metabolism

Digestion

Molecular Genetics

Musculoskeletal System

Respiration

Circulation

Homeostasis

Endocrine System

Nervous System

Thermochemistry

Thermodynamics

Redox Reactions

Isomers

Aromatic Compounds

Ketones

Aldehydes

Peptides

Spectroscopy

Next Steps:

If you truly want to be a doctor, talk to one. Politely ask about one or two topics from this section.

VΓ⦉

LAW

Among many things, lawyers know all about political science. Would you like to be a lawyer? Here's your starting point!

Words Lawyers Commonly Use

Evidence

Information, material, or testimony presented in court or during a legal proceeding that is used to establish facts relevant to the case.

Valid

Something that is legally binding and enforceable. For example, a valid contract is one that meets all the legal requirements for formation and is enforceable by law.

Contract

A legally binding agreement between two or more parties that creates obligations and rights enforceable by law. It typically involves an offer, acceptance, consideration, and mutual intent to be bound.

Ethical

Conduct that is in accordance with professional standards and principles of fairness, honesty, and integrity. Lawyers are bound by ethical rules and

codes of professional conduct that govern their
behavior and interactions with clients, colleagues,
and the court.

Case

A legal dispute or controversy brought before a
court of law for resolution. It involves parties
with opposing interests seeking a decision or
judgment from the court on a particular legal issue
or claim.

Obligation

A legal duty or responsibility to perform a certain
act or to refrain from doing something. It can arise
from a contract, statute, or common law principles,
and failure to fulfill an obligation can result in
legal consequences.

Petition

A formal written request or application submitted to
a court or other authority seeking specific relief
or action. It typically sets forth the facts and
legal arguments supporting the request and asks the
court to grant the requested relief.

History to Boost Your Credibility

Date | Event

Date	Event
1776:	Declaration of Independence
1787:	Constitution of the United States of America
1794:	Whiskey Rebellion
1803:	Louisiana Purchase
1815:	Battle of New Orleans
1823:	Monroe Doctrine
1829:	Era of the Common Man
1848:	Treaty of Guadalupe Hidalgo
1857:	Dred Scott decision
1861:	The Civil War
1863:	Battle of Gettysburg
1876:	Battle of the Little Bighorn
1886:	Haymarket Affair
1896:	Plessy v. Ferguson
1914:	World War I
1939:	World War II
1944:	Operation Overlord (D-Day)
1945:	Battle of Iwo Jima
1945:	Battle of Okinawa
1950:	Korean War
1964:	Vietnam War
1991:	Operation Desert Storm
2001:	September 11 attacks
2003:	Operation Iraqi Freedom
2011:	Operation Neptune Spear

Commonly Expressed Centuries:

Century	Year
16th Century	1501-1600 (also called "the 1500s")
17th Century	1601-1700 (also called "the 1600s")
18th Century	1701-1800 (also called "the 1700s")
19th Century	1801-1900 (also called "the 1800s")
20th Century	1901-2000
21st Century	2001-present

Next Steps:

If you truly want to be a lawyer, research the following calculated questions:

- Under common law, what elements are needed to create a valid contract?
- If false evidence is submitted in a case, what are the lawyer's ethical obligations?
- In contract law, what is the legal term for the withdrawal of an offer before it is accepted?
- What is the legal term for the failure of one party to fulfill their obligations under a contract?

VOODOO

Awesome Sauce: Terms and Idioms

Humble pie

Example:

I ate humble pie after my little brother taught me how to fly.

Run for the hills

Example:

If you stumble into a wasp nest, run for the hills.

Making peanuts

Example:

Tybalt, who mowed all the lawns in his neighborhood for a measly $2, is making peanuts.

Bogus

Example:

Sal failed to complete his chemistry assignment and leveraged a bogus "family emergency" excuse when questioned by his professor the next day.

Gobbledygook

Example:

Mercutio didn't study his rocket science homework, so his answers on the exam were utter gobbledygook.

Fortnight

Example:

At dinner, Timothy quickly devours pizza, but it takes a fortnight for him to approach the broccoli dish.

Jack squat

Example:

Reginald has done jack squat on his assignments, and he hasn't practiced his piano either!

Tacky

Example:

Bartholomew made the tacky decision to wear his sunglasses at the dinner table, and his cousin called him "tasteless."

Take it with a grain of salt

Example:

As Porphyry listened to the prisoner explain how to become the president of the United States, he took the advice with a grain of salt.

Spill the beans

Example:

It's 23:00, and the entire apartment complex can hear your music! Whose poor decision was this party? Spill the beans. Don't just stand there speechless!

Subpar

Example:

If 70% is the minimum passing score, then earning 60% is subpar.

Slack

Example:

Romeo begged for an assignment extension, but his English teacher refused to cut him any slack.

Flack

Example:

I made a poor decision to babysit Horatio and his brothers. They shredded the entire house, and now I'm likely to catch flack from their parents.

Flak

Example:

Our heroic fighter pilots dodged the terrifying flak as they soared over the English Canal.

⊓⌐⌐⌉<

Calculated Questions

This is a compilation of all questions from each of the "Next Steps" sections.

- How does a rocket scientist use a periodic table?
- Why are some metals liquid?
- When will a solid turn directly to a gas, and what is this process called?
- What are ionic bonds, and how are they different from metallic bonds?
- How do we predict the behavior of complex molecules and reactions?
- Relative to sound, how fast is Mach 3?
- What's the purpose of a pre-flight inspection?
- When does a pilot fly with instruments only?
- How do we avoid hot mics?
- As you approach an airport to land the plane, who must you communicate with?
- In the event of catastrophic engine failure, many planes can glide safely to the ground. How does that work?
- Under common law, what elements are needed to create a valid contract?
- If false evidence is submitted in a case, what are the lawyer's ethical obligations?

- In contract law, what is the legal term for the withdrawal of an offer before it is accepted?
- What is the legal term for the failure of one party to fulfill their obligations under a contract?

Addendum

Arabic	Roman Numeral
1	I
2	II
3	III
4	IV
5	V
6	VI
7	VII
8	VIII
9	IX
10	X
11	XI
12	XII
13	XIII
14	XIV
15	XV
16	XVI
17	XVII
18	XVIII
19	XIX
20	XX
21	XXI
22	XXII

23	XXIII
24	XXIV
30	XXX
40	XL
50	L
60	LX
70	LXX
80	LXXX
90	XC
100	C

A | B | C J | K | L

D | E | F M | N | O

G | H | I P | Q | R

 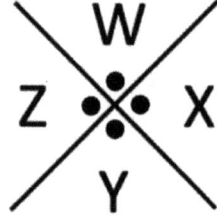

S
V   T
U

W
Z   X
Y

www.ingramcontent.com/pod-product-compliance
Lightning Source LLC
Chambersburg PA
CBHW051709020426
42333CB00014B/913